Food for our Times

an anthology of recipes donated
in aid of Oxfam

Introduction by Delia Smith
Illustrations by Anna MacMiadhachain
Photographs by Norman Hollands

HODDER AND STOUGHTON
LONDON   SYDNEY   AUCKLAND   TORONTO

British Library Cataloguing in Publication Data
Food for our times
    1 Cookery.
    I Oxfam
    641.5   TX717

ISBN 0 340 22568 8

Foreword from Oxfam

In this divided world there are few things which unite us all – food has to be one of them. This book was born out of the belief that the top cookery experts of our time could be brought together to share with us all some of their favourite and most economical recipes, and at the same time raise money to help those in great need.

The result is a fascinating mixture of recipes from many countries which should give great pleasure to many people. It will also bring happiness to families in some of the poorest parts of the world as, owing to the generosity of all the contributors and the publisher, a large sum of money is to be raised from it to help Oxfam's work overseas.

It might seem rather strange that Oxfam should be involved with such a project, but in fact one of the fundamental aims of Oxfam is for the production and proper use of food. The reasons are obvious, but can never be stated enough. In the Western world food is taken for granted, misused and wasted – up to twenty-five per cent is physically thrown away in this country alone – whilst at the same time in the Third World over 500 million people are chronically under-nourished.

This is not to suggest simplistic answers, but the fact remains that positive and practical action is being taken to effect change. All the money raised from this book will go to help people in the poorest parts of the world grow and make better use of food. It will not revolutionise the world, but it will make a crucial difference to hundreds, if not thousands of families.

Oxfam would like to express its deep appreciation to all those concerned with the project – all the contributors, especially Delia Smith, the publisher, and of course, you the reader.

Introduction

For a cookery writer there is an apparent contradiction in spending one's life dreaming up new recipes – and persuading people to cook them – when the harsh fact is that the majority of people in this world have barely enough food to keep them at subsistence level, and many even less than that.

I often wonder whether these two things are reconcilable, and the conclusion I come to is that we in this relatively affluent country have two distinct responsibilities. The first is obviously to try to help poorer countries in whatever way we can, and not least by supporting agencies such as OXFAM, whose inspiring work surely needs no elaboration here. And the other is to treat our own resources – and food above all – with care and respect and even with imagination.

It is easy to take our food for granted when it floods the supermarket shelves, when it comes packeted, tinned, frozen and needs little or no preparation. But more and more we are being confronted with signs that Britain is far from immune to the effects of world shortages or over-exploitation. Increasingly, I feel, we shall have to re-assess our way of eating (and cooking), to make wider use of unfamiliar ingredients, to make more responsible use of those we have always taken for granted.

This is one of the underlying principles of this book – hence the title: FOOD FOR OUR TIMES. I believe another is to make the collective point, by many leading cooks, restaurateurs and cookery writers who have enthusiastically donated their recipes to this book, that food on this overpopulated planet *is* precious. We needn't feel guilty about having good food, but we should make the most of it and cook it *well*. Finally it goes without saying that by buying this book you will help a little towards the good work of OXFAM. So, please, don't just read this, buy it and get cooking!

List of Colour Plates

Contents

9

13

Conversion tables

WEIGHTS

½ oz	10 g (grams)
1	25
1½	40
2	50
2½	60
3	75
4	110
4½	125
5	150
6	175
7	200
8	225
9	250
10	275
12	350
1 lb	450
1½	700
2	900
3	1 kg 350 g

VOLUME

2 fl oz	55 ml
3 fl oz	75
5 fl oz (¼ pint)	150
½ pint	275
¾ pint	425
1 pint	570
1¾ pints	1 litre
(2 pint basin = 1 litre)	

TEMPERATURES

Mark 1	275 F	140 C
2	300	150
3	325	170
4	350	180
5	375	190
6	400	200
7	425	220
8	450	230

MEASUREMENTS

⅛ in	3 mm (millimetre)
¼ in	½ cm (centimetre)
½	1
¾	2
1	2.5
1¼	3
1½	4
1¾	4.5
2	5
3	7.5
4	10
5	13
6	15
7	18
8	20
9	23
10	25.5
11	28
12	30

All these are *approximate* conversions, which have been either rounded up or down. In a few recipes it has been necessary to modify them very slightly.

Soups and Starters

Cream of Chestnut Soup (Serves 4)

Made ahead of time and needing no last minute attention, this subtle flavoured soup can be made with 11 oz dried chestnuts (300 g) soaked overnight, but it is worth all the effort of peeling fresh chestnuts.

9 oz chestnuts (250 g)
1¾ pints light stock (vegetable or chicken) (1 litre)
2½ oz butter or margarine (60 g)
½ a small onion
1 tablespoon flour
2 sticks celery
seasoning
2 tablespoons cream

Make a small cut in each end of the chestnuts, drop them in to boiling water for 10 minutes. Remove the outer and inner skins and place in a pan with half the butter and just enough stock to cover; simmer for 45–50 minutes. When soft, rub through a fine strainer and work to a smooth purée in the liquidiser.

Melt the remaining butter in a saucepan, add the onion, finely chopped, and cook until soft and golden; blend in the flour. Add the stock and stir until boiling. Add the chestnut purée, the sliced celery and seasoning and simmer for 20 minutes. Adjust the seasoning.

Place the cream in a hot tureen and pour the boiling soup through a strainer on to the cream.

Stir just before serving with fried croûtons of bread handed separately.

Rosemary Hume

Creamy Winter's Soup

(Serves 6–8)

This velvety soup, made from midwinter vegetables, has an unexpectedly subtle flavour which you would guess came from more luxurious ingredients.

2 large carrots
1 lb turnips (450 g)
1 heaped tablespoon plain flour
2½–3 pints chicken or veal stock and milk (use a cube for the stock
    if you have none made) (approximately 1.5 litres)
6–8 oz carton single cream (200 ml)
juice of ½ a lemon
2–3 teaspoons mild French mustard
salt, black pepper

Scrape the carrots and chop them into small cubes. Boil them in salted water for about 5 minutes. Drain and put on one side. Peel the turnips and chop up roughly. Melt the butter in a large saucepan and stir the turnip chunks round in the butter. Stir in the flour. Add the stock and milk and mustard. Bring to the boil, stirring often, then cover the pan and simmer gently for ½ an hour or more until the turnips are really soft. Cool slightly and then whizz up in the liquidiser until creamy, or if you don't have a liquidiser put through a fine Mouli. Put the soup into a saucepan, stir in the cream, gradually stir in the lemon juice, and add salt and pepper to taste. Add the cooked carrot cubes and reheat to serve. Some chopped fresh chives or parsley at the last moment is a pretty addition.

Josceline Dimbleby

Butterbean Soup

(Serves 6–8)

Pulses make nourishing and warming soups. Lentils, green split peas and butterbeans are my favourites for keeping in the store-cupboard. You only need a few vegetables to turn any one into a delicious soup and in this recipe carrot, celery and a little concentrated tomato purée do the job perfectly.

2 oz butter (50 g)
1 large onion
2 carrots
2 stalks celery
2 medium potatoes
8 oz butterbeans, soaked overnight in cold water (225 g)
3 pints water (1.7 litres)
2 chicken stock cubes
1 bay leaf
salt and freshly milled pepper
1 x 2½ oz tin concentrated tomato purée (60 g)

Melt the butter in a large saucepan and add the peeled and coarsely chopped onion. Scrape and cut up the carrots and wash and cut up the celery. Peel and cut the potatoes into dice. Add the carrots, celery and potato and toss in the hot butter and onion. Add the butterbeans (drained from the soaking water). Now stir in the water in the recipe, crumble in the chicken stock cube, add the bay leaf, a seasoning of salt and pepper and the concentrated tomato purée. Bring to a simmer and cover with a lid. Cook gently for about 1 hour or until the butterbeans are squashy and soft—taste one to test as butterbeans can still have a hard centre even though they feel soft on the outside.

Push the cooked vegetables, butterbeans and liquid from the pot through a soup Mouli or, for a smoother mixture, blend to a purée in a liquidiser. Return to the soup pan, check seasoning and reheat. This soup is nice served with a garnish of white bread cut in tiny cubes and fried to a crisp golden brown in hot butter.

Katie Stewart.

Goulash Soup

(Serves 4–6)

½ lb shin of beef (225 g)
2 teaspoons flour
2 large onions
1½ oz lard (40 g)
1 teaspoon paprika
1 teaspoon caraway seeds
1 tablespoon vinegar
salt and pepper
a little fresh or dried marjoram if possible
about 2 pints water (1.15 litres)
2 medium sized potatoes

Cut the meat into small dice, free of fat or gristle, and roll it in the flour. Slice the onions thinly and fry them in the melted lard, till they are soft and a good colour. Brown the diced meat all over.

Blend in the paprika and any remaining flour. Add the seasoning and the warm water. Simmer very gently till the meat is soft—about 1 hour if you have chopped it fairly small.

Add the potatoes, peeled and diced, and simmer till they are tender—about 15 minutes longer. This soup should be a lovely brownish-red. If it is too pallid, colour it with a little concentrated tomato purée. The soup is excellent without the caraway seeds if you do not like their flavour.

Margaret Costa

Jerusalem Artichoke Soup (Serves 6)

Sometimes called Palestine Soup, this is an excellent way of using Jerusalem artichokes, one of our most underrated winter vegetables.

2 lb Jerusalem artichokes (1 kg)
1 oz butter (25 g)
4 oz chopped onion (100 g)
2 oz diced celery (50 g)
4 pints chicken stock (2.5 litres)
¼ pint double cream (150 ml)
salt, pepper

Jerusalem artichokes come into season in November—when there is also good quality celery in the shops—so this is a soup for the winter months. You can peel the artichokes, but it isn't essential for this dish; simply scrub and blanch them for 5 minutes in boiling salted water. Then cut them into thin slices and prepare the onion and celery.

Melt the butter in a pan and fry the vegetables gently for about 10 minutes until they are soft, but not coloured. Then transfer the vegetables to a large saucepan, add the stock and seasoning, and simmer for about 20 minutes. By this time the soup should start to thicken as the vegetables soften. Rub the mixture through a sieve or liquidize until you have a smooth soup. Return to the pan and stir in the cream, check the seasoning and simmer for 5 minutes before serving. Make sure that the soup does not boil.

Garnish the soup with crushed, toasted hazelnuts, which should be plentiful, at least before Christmas.

David Mabey

Turnep Soup

(Serves 6)

What could be cheaper or easier: its rich nutty flavour and amber colour quickly win over those who despise this treasured root.

1½ lb turnip (weighed when peeled) (700 g)
2 oz butter (50 g)
2 pints chicken stock (use cubes if necessary) (1.15 litres)
2 oz dry (not stale) brown bread (50 g)
1 tablespoon olive oil
1 level teaspoon ground nutmeg
salt

Cut the turnips into 1 inch (2.5 cm) cubes. Melt the butter, swirling it round the pan until lightly brown and nutty.

Add onions and allow to soften. Add turnips, cover the pan and gently allow the vegetables to soften over a low heat. This will take approximately 20–25 minutes.

Cut the bread into ½ inch (1 cm) cubes. Heat the oil in frying pan and fry the bread until crisp and evenly browned. Add fried bread to softened turnip and onion. Add stock. Simmer for a further 20 minutes. Season boldly with salt and plenty of nutmeg.

Pass through a blender leaving the texture somewhat 'tweedy'.

Curried Parsnip Soup (Serves 6)

There is not much invention in cookery—mainly additions, alterations, adjustments, importations—so I feel a modest pride in this recipe I made up for an *Observer Magazine* article in 1969. It was reprinted in *Good Things*.

1 large or 2 medium parsnips
4 oz chopped onion (110 g)
1 large clove garlic, finely chopped
2–3 oz butter (50–75 g)
1 rounded teaspoon curry powder
1 tablespoon flour
2 pints hot beef stock (1 litre)
¼ pint cream or top of the milk (150 ml)
chives, salt, pepper

Peel and slice the parsnip, then cut it into chunks, removing any very hard core. Put it into a pan with the onion, garlic and butter. Cook slowly for 10 minutes, covered, giving the vegetables an occasional stir to mix them up well with the butter. They should not brown at all. Add curry powder and flour and stir about for 2 minutes. Pour in enough of the beef stock to cover the vegetables. Cover and leave until tender. Liquidise or put through the Mouli-légumes, adding the rest of the beef stock and a little extra water if necessary to dilute the consistency further. Reheat, keeping the soup just under boiling point. Stir in the cream and chives with salt, and pepper if you think the flavour needs rousing—usually the curry powder provides enough pepperiness.

Serve with croûtons of bread fried in butter.

Jane Grigson

Chicken and Tomato Soup (Serves 6)

This is a simple soup to make, but it has a beguiling tart/sweet flavour. It is often made in Jewish kitchens with leftover chicken soup but it is equally good with giblet stock or bouillon cubes.

2 pints chicken stock (1 litre)
15 oz can peeled plum tomatoes (450 g)
juice of a large lemon
2 level tablespoons brown sugar
4 level tablespoons canned or tubed tomato purée
2 level tablespoons rice

Put all the ingredients except the rice into a soup pan. (Sieve the tomatoes or not as you prefer.) Bring to the boil, then add the rice. Cover and simmer for 30 minutes. Taste and add additional sugar or lemon juice if necessary.

Evelyn Rose

Watercress Soup

(Serves 4)

This is one of my favourite soups and it's very quick to make—with a pressure cooker it can be made in about 15 minutes from start to finish. The trick is to leave the skins on the potatoes as this greatly improves the flavour (as well as nourishment) of the soup. After liquidising, the soup is sieved to give a smooth texture.

1 bunch of watercress
1 lb potatoes, in their skins, scrubbed (450 g)
1 onion, peeled
1 oz butter (25 g)
1½ pints water or light vegetable stock (900 ml)
¼ pint single cream or top of the milk (150 ml)
sea salt
freshly ground black pepper

Wash the watercress carefully. Cut off the stalk ends and chop; chop the leaves separately. Cut the potato into small cubes and slice the onion. Melt the butter in a large saucepan (or pressure cooker), add the potato and onion and cook gently for 5 minutes, stirring frequently, then add the chopped watercress stalks and cook for a further 2–3 minutes. Stir in the water or stock, bring up to the boil, then half cover saucepan with a lid (or put top on pressure cooker) and simmer soup for 15–20 minutes (or cook for 5 minutes under 15 lb pressure) until vegetables are tender. Liquidise, then pass mixture through a sieve. Return to saucepan, add cream or top of the milk and chopped watercress leaves. Season with salt and black pepper to taste. Reheat, but do not boil.

Rose Elliot

Avocado and Cucumber Soup

(Serves 4)

In the summer I get hooked on cold soups; light, cool to look at and usually with a pleasant lemony overtone. Serve cold soup in bowls that have been chilled in the refrigerator so that everything is iceberg cold.

2 ripe avocados
juice of ½ a lemon
½ a cucumber
1½ pints milk (850 ml)
1 beef stock cube dissolved in 2 tablespoons boiling water
1 teaspoon grated onion
3 tablespoons sour cream or yoghurt
1 tablespoon chopped chives

Peel avocados and remove stones. Sprinkle at once with lemon juice. Combine avocados, cucumber (peeled and cut into small pieces) and milk and purée through a fine food mill or in an electric liquidiser. Add stock cube and water. Add onion, blend in cream or yoghurt and season with salt and pepper. Chill well and serve cold with a sprinkling of chopped chives on each portion.

Marika Hanbury Tenison

Melon and Cassia Bud Salad (Serves 6)

You may find cassia buds a little hard to get if your local herbalist does not stock them. But they are not dissimilar to cinnamon in flavour, so use the latter if the buds are not available.

1 honeydew melon
4 oz caster sugar (110 g)
2 tablespoons water
rind of a small orange
1 teaspoon crushed cassia buds or powdered cinnamon
1 tablespoon orange flower water

Put sugar, water, cassia buds or cinnamon, orange flower water and rind into a pan. Simmer until syrupy, but not caramelised. Cut top off melon about 3 inches down (7.5 cm). Scoop out the seeds. Then with a melon baller scoop out the flesh (or use a teaspoon).

Put the melon balls into the syrup, leave to cool, fill back into the melon shell and chill for 4 hours.

Decorate with orange segments and angelica spikes.

Pears with Mustard Cream Mayonnaise

(Serves 4)

This is such an easy starter but it depends on the pears not only being perfectly ripe but blemish-free. If you like a sharp mayonnaise, whisk the lemon juice, used to prevent the pears discolouring, into the mayonnaise with the mustard and cream.

2 beautifully ripe eating pears
1 tablespoon lemon juice
4 tablespoons home-made mayonnaise
1 tablespoon made Dijon mustard
2 tablespoons whipped double cream
a few nice lettuce leaves
a few blanched almonds

Peel the pears keeping them a good shape, then using a teaspoon, scoop out the cores. Brush each pear half with the lemon juice to prevent discolouration. Whisk the mayonnaise with the mustard and double cream and add 1 teaspoon boiling water if it is too thick to coat the pears smoothly. Rinse and dry the lettuce leaves and arrange them on 4 small plates. Put a pear half, cut side down, on each plate and coat it with a little of the mustard cream mayonnaise. Split the almonds and grill them until they are golden brown, moving them around under the grill all the time. Allow to cool, then use to garnish the pears.

Kathie Webber

Avocado Cucumber Canapés (Serves 6)

Some years ago I gave a series of demonstrations using Caribbean foods. All sorts of exotic ingredients were flown in so that I met breadfruit and ackees and other unknown ingredients. I was delighted to find a selection of simple recipes based on avocados from this part of the world. The following canapés make an excellent vegetarian dish or can be served with drinks.

Makes about 20 cocktail canapés or serves 6 as an hors d'oeuvre.

2 large ripe avocados
a shake of cayenne pepper
a shake of salt
juice of 2 lemons
a few drops of Tabasco sauce
a few drops of olive oil
1 large cucumber
red pepper to garnish

Halve the avocados, take out the stones and scoop the pulp from the skins into a basin. Blend with the seasonings and half the lemon juice immediately, to ensure the avocado does not lose its colour. Add the sauce and oil. Thinly slice the cucumber—do this diagonally to give rather larger slices. Sprinkle with the remaining lemon juice and season. Arrange on a large flat dish. Top with the avocado purée. Cut the pepper into thin strips, discarding the seeds and core. Place on top of the avocado mixture. For the canapés the cucumber slices should be put on to tiny rounds of buttered rye bread.

Marguerite Patten

Caviar d'Aubergines

(Serves 6)

4 large aubergines
2 Spanish onions, finely chopped
2 cloves garlic, crushed
¼ teaspoon oregano
5–6 tablespoons chopped parsley
6 tablespoons olive oil
2 x 14 oz cans tomatoes, drained and chopped (2 x 400 g)
salt and freshly ground black pepper
a generous pinch of sugar
6 small olives, pitted and halved

Pre-heat the oven to moderate, gas mark 4 (350 °F, 180 °C).

Bake the aubergines for about 20 minutes. Meanwhile in a saucepan sauté the onions, garlic, oregano and 4 tablespoons chopped parsley in olive oil until the onions are soft and golden. Add the tomatoes and simmer for about 5 minutes longer until the ingredients have amalgamated into a sauce.

When the aubergines are soft, peel off their skins; drain the pulp thoroughly and chop finely. Stir the aubergine pulp into the tomato mixture; season with salt, freshly ground black pepper and sugar and simmer for about 10 minutes longer, stirring until well blended. Turn the mixture into a shallow serving dish and allow to cool.

Serve cold, garnished with the remaining parsley and pitted, halved black olives.

Runner Beans à la Grecque (Serves 4–6)

Serve this dish as an appetiser, either lukewarm or cold, with plenty of good bread to soak up the delicious juices.

2½ lb runner beans (1.25 kg)
salt
1 large Spanish onion, finely chopped
4 large ripe tomatoes, peeled and chopped
6 tablespoons finely chopped parsley
4–6 tablespoons olive oil
2 teaspoons sugar
freshly ground black pepper

Top, tail and string the beans, and slice them thinly lengthwise. Put the beans in a colander and sprinkle them generously with salt, rubbing it in gently between the palms of your hands. Put the beans aside for an hour or so to wilt and soften.

Rinse the beans thoroughly under the cold tap, shaking the colander to rid them of as much moisture as possible.

In a heavy pan, combine the beans with the onion, tomatoes, parsley and oil. Sprinkle with sugar to taste and a generous grinding of pepper. Add just enough boiling water to cover. Bring to simmering point and cook gently, with the lid half on, for 30 minutes, or until the beans are tender and the sauce rich and reduced. Cool. A tablespoon of fresh olive oil may be stirred in at the end for extra flavour.

When the beans are cool, correct seasoning with salt, more sugar or pepper and serve lukewarm or cold.

Helena Radecka

Plaice and Cucumber Starter (Serves 4)

I first had a recipe similar to this one at a rather large dinner party. Not knowing my hostess very well I didn't like to ask for the recipe so I experimented to 'reproduce' the dish. The original had prawns in it, but plaice, haddock or even the thin end of a cod fillet can be used.

1 small plaice, filleted
1 level tablespoon plain flour
salt and freshly ground black pepper
1 cucumber
4 oz button mushrooms (110 g)
1½ oz butter (40 g)
2 teaspoons soya sauce
3 tablespoons chicken stock
3 tablespoons single cream
chopped fresh herbs to garnish

Remove skin from plaice fillets, cut fillets across in thin strips and toss in the flour which has been well seasoned with salt and pepper. Wash cucumber, cut 4 thin slices and reserve for the garnish. Cut remainder into ½ inch (1 cm) dice. Cook in boiling salted water for 3 minutes. Drain and rinse quickly with cold water. Wash, trim and thinly slice the mushrooms. Melt half the butter in a saucepan and fry strips of plaice gently until lightly browned. Remove from pan and drain on kitchen paper. Melt remaining butter in a pan, add mushrooms and fry for 2 minutes. Add cucumber, cover and simmer for about 2 minutes. Stir in soya sauce, chicken stock and cream. Bring to the boil. Return fish to pan and heat through gently. Adjust seasoning and spoon into small warmed dishes. Garnish each with a twist of cucumber and a sprinkle of fresh herbs.

Mussels in White Wine Sauce

(Serves 6)

It is extremely important to clean the mussels thoroughly; in order to make this easier, place the mussels in cold water to cover in the sink or in a large bowl. Into this add 2 tablespoons natural oatmeal and leave to soak for 2 hours, ideally for 4 hours. The mussels eat this and discard their sand, so it makes removing the barnacles and beards far easier, taking only about 30 minutes. Mussels are cheap and rich in protein, and this dish may be prepared ahead of time up to the placing under the grill at the last minute. Serve each person 4 mussels, but order more that you require as there are always some mussels which do not open when cooked, so must be discarded. There are approximately 25 mussels in 1 quart (1.15 litres), which is 2 lb (900 g) in weight.

2½ lb mussels (1.15 kg)
1 onion, chopped fine
2 shallots, chopped fine
2 cloves garlic, chopped fine
8 fl oz dry white wine (225 ml)

For the white wine sauce:
1 shallot, chopped fine
1 clove garlic, chopped fine
2 oz unsalted butter (50 g)
2 tablespoons plain flour
reserved mussel liquid
¾ pint milk (450 ml)
2 egg yolks
4 fl oz double cream (100–125 ml)

Place mussels, onion, shallots, garlic and wine in a deep saucepan, bring to the boil and steam until mussels open. Discard any which have not opened. Drain mussels, straining and reserving the liquid. Discard one half of each mussel shell and place in a roasting pan on a bed of rock salt which has been heated in the pan to keep warm. Make the sauce. Place the shallot and garlic in the butter in a saucepan and sauté until transparent, stir in the flour, then add the reserved mussel liquid and milk to make the sauce smooth. Reduce. Beat egg yolks and cream together and add to the sauce. Heat through *but do not boil*. Pour sauce over each mussel and place under the grill for a few minutes to brown, then transfer to a serving dish. Serve immediately.

Potato Sausages

(Saucisses de Pommes de Terre)   (Serves 4)

Here is an admirable cheap little recipe, and quite an old one (it appears with variations in several early nineteenth century French books) for using up leftover meat or chicken.

3–4 tablespoons meat, cooked and finely chopped (chicken, turkey, kidney, calf's head, brains)
½ oz butter (10 g)
2 shallots, chopped
parsley
2–3 tablespoons stock
1 teaspoon flour or potato flour
2 eggs
4 large potatoes, boiled in their skins
butter, salt, pepper

Melt the butter with the shallots and a little chopped parsley. Stir in the meat and add the stock, then stir in the flour or potato flour. Let it reduce, season, then add the well-beaten eggs. Stir until the mixture starts to thicken, and then take quickly from the fire before it turns to scrambled eggs.

Peel the potatoes and mash very smooth with a little butter, salt and pepper, but no milk. Into this purée incorporate the meat mixture and beat again until it is all well amalgamated.

Spread thickly on a lightly buttered plate and leave to get quite cold, preferably until next day. Take little spoonfuls of the mixture and, on a well-floured board, roll them and shape them into little sausages, no larger than small chipolatas or cocktail sausages. Fry them, not too fast, in good clear beef dripping or clarified butter, turning them over once or twice until they are golden and crisp on each side. Take them out, as they are done, with a perforated spoon.

Serve them very hot as a first course with, if you like, a freshly made tomato sauce, but they are also excellent on their own.

Elizabeth David

Chicken Liver and Caper Pâté

(Serves 6–8)

This is extremely easy to make, at the most it takes 30 minutes to prepare with the minimum of cooking. Put in a pretty pot it is attractive on the table. It can also be prepared ahead and frozen or just placed in the refrigerator for 12 hours. If you haven't any Cognac, add more sherry. The capers are important as they add some texture to an otherwise smooth pâté.

1 lb chicken livers (450 g)
3 shallots, chopped fine
4 oz unsalted butter (110 g)
1½ tablespoons Cognac
1½ tablespoons sherry
2 teaspoons salt
¼ teaspoon nutmeg
¼ teaspoon black pepper
a pinch each of thyme, basil and marjoram
half of a 3 oz bottle of capers (half a 75 g bottle)
3–4 tablespoons clarified butter (see below)

Sauté the chicken livers and the shallots in the butter for 2 to 4 minutes or until the livers are browned on the outside but pink inside. Transfer to a bowl. Stir the sherry and Cognac into the butter remaining in the pan and pour over the livers. Season with salt, nutmeg, pepper and herbs. Combine well and purée the mixture, about a third at a time, in a blender or food processor. Add the capers, but do not blend, so that they give a slightly rough texture to the pâté. Spoon into an earthenware terrine or ramekin, cover the surface with clarified butter and chill for 12 hours. Serve with hot buttered toast.

Clarified butter
In a heavy saucepan melt butter over low heat. Allow butter to rest for 2 or 3 minutes away from the heat and skim the froth off

the top. Pour the clear butter carefully through a muslin-lined sieve into a small bowl, leaving the milky solids at the bottom of the saucepan. 8 oz (225 g) butter yields about 6 oz (175 g) clarified butter.

Thomas's Pâté   (Serves 12)

2 medium onions, quartered
1 lb pigs' liver (450 g)
1 lb pork sausagemeat (450 g)
3 level tablespoons chopped parsley
1½ level teaspoons salt
freshly ground black pepper
1 clove garlic, crushed
8 rashers streaky bacon

Mince the onion and liver until smooth and mix with the sausagemeat, parsley, seasoning and garlic.

De-rind the bacon and stretch with the back of a knife until twice the length. Use to line the base and sides of a 2 lb, 9 x 4 x 2½ inch (900 g, 23 x 10 x 6 cm) loaf tin.

Pile the meat mixture into the tin and level the top. Cover with foil and stand in a roasting tin with 1 inch of water (2.5 cm) in the base. Cook at gas mark 3 (325 °F, 170 °C) for 1½ hours. Leave to cool in the tin. Turn out when quite cold.

Mary Berry.

Rabbit and Lemon Terrine (Serves 15)

½ lb streaky bacon (225 g)
½ lb chicken livers (225 g)
2 cloves garlic, crushed
1 small onion, grated
12 oz lean pork, minced (350 g)
juice and rind of 1 small lemon
1 teaspoon French mustard
salt and black pepper
a few sprigs of fresh tarragon
12 oz uncooked rabbit (fresh or frozen), cut into strips (350 g)
1 large onion, cut into rings
½ pint dry white wine (275 ml)
celery leaves

Remove rinds from bacon and stretch with the back of a knife. Line a pâté dish or terrine with bacon. Wash, trim and finely chop the livers. Chop most of the tarragon, reserving some unchopped for the garnish. Mix the livers with the garlic, onion, pork, lemon juice and rind, seasoning and chopped tarragon. Pack a third of this mixture into the base of the terrine. Cover with layer of rabbit, well seasoned, and onion rings. Add another layer of pork mixture, then more rabbit and onion, then a final layer of pork. Pour the wine over and cover with foil. Bake in a bain marie at gas mark 3 (325 °F, 170 °C) for about 2 hours until firm. Place a weight on top and leave for an hour before skimming off any fatty liquid. Chill. Garnish with sprigs of fresh tarragon and celery leaves.

Alex Baker

Eggs, Cheese and Pasta

Portuguese Omelettes   (Serves 2)

2 slices white bread
grated Parmesan cheese
parsley
cayenne pepper
salt
6 eggs
butter

Cut the bread into small cubes and fry them in butter to make
croûtons. Put some of the cheese, chopped parsley and cayenne
pepper into a paper bag and shake the croûtons in it.
    Make a runny omelette, put the croûtons in the middle and
fold it over. Sprinkle the rest of the cheese and parsley mixture
on top and serve straightaway.

Caroline Conran.

Eggs Unlimited

A quick and simple dish that can be adapted to feed as many
people as desired.

dry sliced bread
sliced cooked ham
sliced cheese (Cheddar, Bel Paese, Gruyère or Mozarella)
black pepper
eggs

Butter a shallow baking tin and line the bottom completely with
sliced dry bread, crusts removed. Cover the bread with a layer
of sliced cooked ham, removing most of the fat. Cover the ham

with a layer of sliced cheese—Cheddar, Bel Paese, Gruyère or Mozarella, according to your taste. Sprinkle with black pepper and cover with as many eggs as you require, sliding them carefully out of their shells to avoid breaking the yolks. Bake for about 15 minutes at gas mark 6 (400 °F, 200 °C) or until the whites of the eggs are just set.

Arabella Boxer.

Cheese Baked Eggs (Serves 4)

The perfect starter to a light main dish, the choice, too, for a tray supper. Deep natural scallop shells, a good buy from the fishmonger, make an attractive alternative to ramekins.

4 large eggs
4 tablespoons double cream
2 oz Cheddar cheese, grated (50 g)
1 tablespoon lemon juice
1 tablespoon dry white wine or cider
1 level teaspoon dry mustard
¼ level teaspoon salt
a pinch of ground black pepper
½ level teaspoon dried basil
1 oz fresh white breadcrumbs (25 g)

Break the eggs into individual buttered ramekins. Mix together the cream, cheese, lemon juice, wine (or cider), mustard, salt and pepper. Cover the eggs with the seasoned cream and sprinkle with the breadcrumbs mixed with basil. Place the dishes in a roasting tin with hot water to come half way up, and bake in the oven at gas mark 5 (375 °F, 190 °C) for 15–20 minutes. Serve at once.

Margaret Coombes.

Oeufs à la Tripe

(Serves 6)

This is a wonderful luncheon dish.

12 hardboiled eggs
3 very large Spanish onions
3 oz butter (75 g)
1 oz flour (30 g)
¾ pint milk (425 ml)
salt, pepper
3–4 tablespoons thick cream
fresh white breadcrumbs
a little extra butter

Skin the onions and slice them very thinly. Melt the butter in a large pan and put in the onions. Let them soften and become creamy over a gentle heat. Stir in the flour, then add the milk gradually to make a smooth, light sauce. Let it cook for 15 minutes over a low heat, stirring from time to time and seasoning with salt and pepper. Meanwhile hardboil the eggs.

Peel and slice the hardboiled eggs. Put them in a large oval gratin dish. Stir the cream into the sauce and pour it over the eggs. Sprinkle breadcrumbs over the top and dot all over with little pieces of butter.

Put under a gentle grill and allow the top to become golden. Serve very hot with a fresh green salad.

Caroline Conran.

Cheddar Eggs

An easy dish with the minimum of ingredients—this recipe is equally as good served for a first course, as a supper dish accompanied by hot crusty bread.

8 oz Cheddar cheese, grated (225 g)
4 tablespoons single cream
4 large eggs
salt and pepper

Lightly butter a shallow ovenproof dish. Spoon in the grated cheese and make 4 depressions in it. Put a spoonful of cream into each space then break an egg on top. Season each egg with salt and pepper and finally sprinkle a little of the cheese over each one. Bake Cheddar Eggs on the centre shelf of a hot oven, gas mark 7 (425 °F, 220 °C) for 15–20 minutes or until the eggs are just set.

If preferred, the dish can be cooked under a pre-heated grill, when it will take about 20–25 minutes.

Janet Warren

Eggs Flamenca
(Huevos à la Flamenca)   (Serves 4)

The Spanish are past masters at assembling interesting and exotic looking dishes out of bits and pieces. This recipe for eggs comes from Andalusia and as its name implies was invented by the gypsies, traditional performers of the flamenco dance. It costs little to prepare and looks impressive. If you have a large shallow earthenware dish, such as those used in Spain, so much the better, or 4 small individual ones are equally suitable. The colour of the earthenware sets off the dish to perfection.

1 coffee cup oil (preferably olive)
2 potatoes
1 onion
1 sweet red pepper
4 slices of lean smoked ham (in Spain serrano ham is used)
½ lb each of cooked peas and green beans (fresh or frozen) (200 g of each)
1 small can asparagus tips (optional; gypsies use wild asparagus)
4 tomatoes, scalded, peeled and chopped
2 tablespoons tomato paste
pepper and salt
8 eggs
8 thin slices of chorizo (Spanish sausage available at most delicatessen)
1 tablespoon chopped parsley

Peel and dice the potatoes. Heat the oil in a large frying pan and fry potatoes gently till golden. Remove and reserve. Chop the onion, de-seed the red pepper and cut into strips, chop two slices of the ham, and fry in the same oil until the onion is transparent. Then add the peas, beans and asparagus, the tomatoes and tomato paste. Stir in the fried potatoes and add about ½ cup water. Season with pepper and salt and stir everything together. Cook gently for about 5 minutes, stirring occasionally. Brush the earthenware dish with oil and pour in the vegetable mixture. Make eight hollows on the surface for the eggs. Break each egg into a cup without damaging the yolk and pour one into each hollow. Arrange the slices of chorizo and the remaining ham cut into triangles over the surface as decoration and sprinkle with chopped parsley. Put into a moderate oven, gas mark 4 (350 °F, 180 °C) for about 15 minutes, or until the egg whites are just set.

Serve in the same dish, accompanied if you like by a green salad and fresh crusty bread.

Anna Macmiaidhachain

Yellow Flower
Egg with Pork

(Serves 4–6)

This should be served with boiled rice and one or two other dishes at a Chinese meal.

4 eggs
½ teaspoon salt
½ lb lean and fat pork (225 g)
6 medium mushrooms
4 stalks young leeks
2 cloves garlic
3 tablespoons vegetable oil
2 tablespoons butter or lard
3 tablespoons good stock
2 tablespoons soya sauce
2 tablespoons dry sherry
1 tablespoon sesame oil (or ⅔ tablespoon peanut butter blended in
     1½ tablespoons vegetable oil)

Beat the eggs lightly with salt. Cut the pork into thin slices, 2 inch by 1 inch (5 cm by 2.5 cm) and the leeks into ½ inch (1 cm) slices. Cut the mushrooms into quarters. Crush and chop the garlic.

Heat the oil in a large frying pan. When hot add the pork and stir-fry over high heat for 2 minutes; add leeks, garlic and mushrooms. Continue to stir-fry over high heat for 2 minutes. Push all the contents in the pan to one side. Add butter or lard into the other side of the pan. When the fat has melted, add the beaten egg. Tilt so that the egg flows evenly over the pan. Push a spoon or spatula through the egg a few times, and remove pan from heat. Allow the egg to set without burning.

When the egg has set, break it up into 1 inch (2.5 cm) pieces. Return the pan to the heat, add stock, sherry, soya sauce and sesame oil. Turn and mix the egg pieces with the pork, leeks and mushrooms. Continue to cook over medium heat for 1½ minutes.

Spanish Onion Tart

(Serves 4–6)

The well-known French quiche is always popular but, if you are tired of this, the Spanish Onion Tart is an excellent alternative.

For the pastry:
8 oz plain flour (225 g)
a pinch of salt
4 oz butter or margarine (110 g)
1 teaspoon lemon juice
water to mix

For the filling:
1 lb onions (½ kg)
6 oz bacon (175 g)
2 eggs
¼ pint milk (150 ml)
seasoning

First make the pastry. Sieve the flour and salt, rub in the fat, then mix with lemon juice and cold water. Roll out and use to line a 9 inch (23 cm) flan dish. Peel and chop the onions finely; de-rind and chop the bacon. Fry the onions and bacon together until soft but not brown—no extra fat should be necessary. Allow to cool, then blend in the beaten eggs and milk. Season to taste. Pour into the uncooked pastry case. Bake for 15–20 minutes in the centre of a hot oven, gas mark 7 (425 °F, 220 °C), then lower the heat to moderate, gas mark 4 (350 °F, 180 °C) for a further 15–20 minutes until the pastry is crisp and the filling set. Serve hot or cold.

Note: 2–3 oz grated cheese (50–75 g) may be added to the filling.

Cauliflower and Bacon Flan (Serves 6–8)

For the pastry:
8 oz plain flour (225 g)
a large pinch of salt
2 oz margarine (50 g)
2 oz lard or white fat (50 g)

For the filling:
1 medium sized cauliflower
1 onion
2 oz margarine (50 g)
1 pint milk (570 ml)
a bouquet garni
2 oz plain flour (50 g)
2 eggs
salt and pepper
4 rashers streaky bacon

First make the pastry. Sift the flour and salt into a mixing bowl, then add the fats, cut into small pieces, and rub these into the flour with the tips of your fingers. Mix with just enough cold water to make a firm dough, then roll the pastry to fit an 11 inch loose-based flan tin (28 cm). Carefully place the pastry in the tin and neaten the edges. Leave in a cool place while preparing the filling.

Remove and discard the large outside leaves from the cauliflower. Pull off any small young leaves, keep these and divide the cauliflower head into small sprigs. Plunge the young leaves and the sprigs into a pan of boiling salted water; bring it back to the boil and cook for 5 minutes, then drain thoroughly and run quickly under the cold tap; this helps to keep the colour.

Meanwhile peel and slice the onion and cook gently, without colouring, in the margarine in a large saucepan. Put the milk into another saucepan with the bouquet garni, bring it slowly to the boil and strain it. Stir the flour into the onion off the heat. Whisk the herb-flavoured milk into this roux then whisk it over a gentle heat until it thickens and comes to the boil. Cool the sauce slightly then beat in the eggs, one at a time. Season the mixture carefully with salt and pepper. Arrange the cauliflower sprigs and young leaves inside the flan, and pour the sauce over the top. Remove the rinds from the rashers of bacon and arrange the bacon round the top of the flan.

Bake in a fairly hot oven, gas mark 6 (400 °F, 200 °C) for about 40 minutes.

Mary Meredith

Spinach and Curd Cheese Topping for Pasta (Serves 4)

This mixture of spinach, light, tangy curd cheese and lemon juice makes a refreshing and contrasting flavoured topping for buttery wholemeal pasta.

2 lb spinach (900 g)
2 teaspoons chopped rosemary
1½ oz butter (40 g)
1 large onion, finely chopped
1 clove garlic, finely chopped
12 oz curd cheese (350 g)
grated rind and juice of 1 lemon

Pasta: 10 oz wholemeal or buckwheat spaghetti or wholemeal pasta rings or noodles, cooked and tossed with butter and Parmesan cheese (275 g)

Break the stems from the spinach. Put the leaves into a saucepan with the rosemary and no more water than clings to them after washing. Cover them and set them on a low heat for 10 minutes, stirring occasionally. Drain the spinach and press down hard to extract as much moisture as possible. Turn it out on to a board and chop finely. Melt the butter in a large frying pan on a low heat. Mix the onion and garlic and cook them until they are just turning golden. Mix in the spinach, cheese and lemon rind and juice and let them all heat through. Serve as soon as you can so the cheese stays soft.

Pasta in Soured Cream Sauce
(Serves 6–8)

A splendid budget styled dish for an informal supper party with crusty bread and a big bowl of cabbage, celery and apple salad.

1 lb pasta cartwheel shapes (450 g)
3 oz butter (75 g)
2 shallots, skinned and chopped
2 level tablespoons flour
¼ pint chicken stock (150 ml)
¼ pint dry white wine or cider (150 ml)
¼ pint soured cream (150 ml)
salt and freshly ground pepper
4 oz button mushrooms, quartered (125 g)
4 oz mature Cheddar cheese (125 g)
1 lb tomatoes, skinned, quartered and seeded (450 g)
2 x 7 oz cans tuna steak, drained (2 x 198 g)
chopped parsley, to garnish

Cook pasta in boiling salted water. For the sauce, melt 2 oz butter (50 g) and sauté the shallots; stir in the flour and cook a few minutes. Gradually add the stock and wine, then bring to the boil, stirring. Reduce the heat and stir in the soured cream. Season to taste. Keep warm over a low heat. Sauté the mushrooms in the rest of the butter. Drain the pasta. Add to it the mushrooms, sauce, cheese and most of the tomato. Toss lightly. Put the flaked tuna in the base of a large hot shallow ovenproof dish, and spoon over the sauce mixture. Scatter reserved tomato over. Reheat in the oven at gas mark 5 (375 °F, 190 °C) for about 15 minutes. Garnish with plenty of chopped parsley.

Note: If wished, prepare a few hours in advance and reheat until almost bubbling.

Margaret Coombes.

Pasta al Pesto

Pasta pundits argue about the authenticity of Parmesan versus Pecorino (Romano in America) cheese, how much garlic, whether pinenuts are allowed, etcetera. Such esoteric nonsense is not for us—the dish is delicious, in any of its forms.

3 cloves garlic
2 large cups basil leaves
3 oz Pecorino or Parmesan cheese, finely grated (75 g)
olive oil
salt, pepper
2 oz pinenuts (50 g)

cooked pasta

In a liquidiser or mortar, grind the garlic and basil together to a paste. Add the cheese, and enough olive oil to double the quantity you have. Add the pinenuts, and salt and pepper to taste. As soon as the pasta is cooked, rinsed and drained, add a tablespoon of pesto for each guest to be served, and mix well.

Prudence Leith.

Wholewheat Spaghetti with a Mushroomy Sauce (Serves 2)

8–10 oz wholewheat spaghetti (or however much 2 people can eat) (225–275 g)
6 slices streaky bacon, rinded and cut into strips
1 onion, diced
1 green pepper, deseeded and diced
½ lb button mushrooms, thinly sliced (225 g)
2 oz can anchovy fillets in oil (50 g)
6–8 black olives, pitted and coarsely chopped
salt and freshly ground black pepper
2–3 tablespoons olive oil
3 tablespoons chopped parsley
grated Parmesan cheese

Fry the bacon strips in a frying pan until shrivelled and crispy—it needs no additional fat adding to the pan. Drain the bacon bits on kitchen paper and leave aside. Gently fry the diced onion and pepper in the fat remaining in the pan. When softened, stir in the mushrooms and anchovy oil, drained from the can. Chop the anchovies and stir these in also. Cover and cook gently for 10 minutes.

Whilst the sauce cooks, boil the pasta in plenty of salted water until al dente and drain in a colander. Quickly add the olive oil and some seasoning to the pan in which the pasta was boiled; toss the spaghetti in it.

Stir the chopped parsley, black olives and reserved bacon bits into the sauce and cook just sufficiently to heat through. Serve the sauce spooned over the pasta, accompanied by grated Parmesan.

Caroline Liddell

Fish

Baked Mullet with Fresh Herbs and Cumin

(Serves 4–6)

An excellent way of cooking a whole fish such as grey mullet or bream which couldn't be easier to prepare.

1 fish—2–3 lb, gutted but with the head left on (1–1.25 kg)
1–2 tomatoes, sliced in rounds
1 lemon, sliced in rounds
a fistful of fresh herbs—rosemary, thyme, marjoram or mint
2–3 teaspoons powdered cumin
oil
salt, black pepper

Lay the fish on a large piece of foil. Rub the fish with oil. Stuff fresh herbs into the stomach. Sprinkle cumin all over the fish and then salt and pepper. Arrange the tomato and lemon slices over and under the fish and wrap up completely in foil. Bake in a preheated oven at gas mark 6 (400 °F, 200 °C) for 40–50 minutes. Unwrap the foil and carefully push the fish on to a serving dish garnished with the tomato and lemon slices. The delicious juice can be poured out of a separate jug or from the serving dish. Serve with boiled potatoes and a green vegetable.

Josceline Dimbleby

Mackerel with Bacon and Pea Purée

(Serves 2)

2 mackerel, about ½ lb (225 g) apiece, gutted
½ lb green split peas (225 g)
¾ pint light chicken stock (425 ml)
1 medium onion, quartered
1 oz butter (25 g)
salt and freshly ground black pepper
4–6 slices unsmoked streaky bacon, rinded
1 oz butter (25 g)
juice of ½ a lemon

Start by preparing the pea purée. Add the onion to the boiling stock and trickle in the split peas in a steady stream so the stock keeps on the boil. Cover and simmer gently for 30 minutes, or until the peas are absolutely tender and only a little liquid remains—boil briskly if there is still more than a tablespoon of stock left. Remove the pan from the heat and rub the contents through a sieve or Mouli. Beat in the butter and season to taste with salt and freshly ground black pepper, then spread the purée on a buttered oval meat dish which will just nicely accommodate the mackerel side by side.

Rinse and wipe the fish with kitchen paper. Season inside and out and slip ½ oz (10 g) butter inside the belly of each fish. Transfer them to lie on top of the pea purée and pour a little lemon juice inside the fish. Stretch and flatten the bacon slices by 'spreading' them out firmly with a broad-bladed knife. Drape over the fish, trimming the slices where necessary. Cover with foil and bake at gas mark 4 (350 °F, 180 °C) for 30 minutes. Uncover and transfer to cook under the grill to crisp both the bacon and fish skins. Serve hot with additional wedges of lemon.

Caroline Liddell

Stuffed Squid

Squid flourish around the shores of Great Britain, and are a good buy. Choose them, for this recipe, with a 6–8 inch sac (15–20 cm); smaller ones are too tender, and burst.

6 squid
1 tablespoon flour
4 medium onions, chopped
4 cloves garlic, finely chopped or crushed
2 oz smoked bacon, chopped (60 g)
5 tablespoons oil, preferably olive
3 oz white breadcrumbs (90 g)
milk or white wine
2 oz (approximately) chopped parsley (60 g)
salt, pepper, sugar
1 medium can of tomatoes

To prepare the squid, pull the head part away from the body: a good deal of the contents of the bag part will come away with the head. Remove the thin purplish skin from the bag—this rubs away easily with the fingers—and fish out the plastic nib-shaped piece from inside the bag. Rinse well. Set aside while you attend to the head and stuffing.

Chop off the tentacles, cut them into ¼ inch (½ cm) pieces or a little less, and put them on a plate. Attached to the remaining debris, the soft white part, you will see a silver-skinned black streak: this is the ink sac. Put three ink sacs (the rest can be discarded with the remaining head part) into a basin with 3 tablespoons of water. Crush them with a wooden spoon to release the black ink, and mix in the flour. Sieve this inky paste into another basin, and keep to thicken and flavour the sauce at the end of the cooking time.

To make the stuffing, cook the tentacles with the onion, garlic, bacon and oil, until very lightly coloured. Set aside a quarter of this for the sauce. Put the rest into a basin, add the breadcrumbs and just enough milk or wine to make a crumbly paste. Do not add so much liquid that it becomes wet—3–4 tablespoons should be enough. Stir in the parsley and seasoning. Fill the squid bags full, and close the openings with wooden cocktail sticks, or sew them up with button thread.

Put the fried onion that you set aside into a large shallow pan, add the canned tomatoes, breaking them up slightly with a spoon, along with their juice. On top lay the stuffed squid in a single layer. Bring to simmering point, add salt, pepper and a very little sugar, cover and cook for 30–40 minutes, turning over the squid every ten minutes. Do not boil hard or the squid will burst; this does not matter from a flavour point of view, but it spoils the appearance.

10 minutes before the squid are cooked, mix in the ink paste. Correct the sauce seasoning. Serve with boiled rice or triangles of fried bread or small new potatoes.

Jane Grigson

Fillets of Plaice with Crusty Cheese Topping (Serves 4)

Any white fish fillets can be used for this dish, but it is especially suitable with small plaice which can often be bought at bargain prices. The topping prevents the fish from drying out and shrinking and also provides a 'built-in' sauce. I give the recipe for four but it is equally successful when halved and cooked in a smaller dish.

fillets from two medium plaice—about 3 lb in all (1.5 kg)
2 oz butter (50 g)
2 tablespoons (approximately) salad cream
4 heaped tablespoons grated Cheddar cheese

Wash the fish, salt it and leave in a colander to drain. 10 minutes before the fish is required, melt the butter under the grill in a dish that is just large enough to hold the fish tightly packed in one layer. Dip each fillet into the melted butter, then turn it over and lay side by side in the dish. Grill gently for 7 minutes, basting once with the buttery juices. Spread with the salad cream, then coat thickly with the grated cheese. Continue to grill for another 3 minutes, or until the cheese has set into a crusty layer and is a rich brown.

Evelyn Rose

Fish Slice

(Serves 4 generously)

The pastry for this is best made the day before it is baked and can be left overnight in a cold place.

For the Quick Flaky Pastry:
8 oz plain flour (225 g)
a good pinch of salt
6 oz margarine, preferably in a hard block from the refrigerator (175 g)
cold water to mix

For the filling:
4 frozen cod steaks (they can be used frozen)
1 oz butter, softened at room temperature (25 g)
1 level tablespoon chopped parsley
salt and pepper
a squeeze of lemon juice

For the glaze:
1 egg yolk beaten with a teaspoon of water and a pinch of salt

Sift the flour and salt into a mixing bowl. Grate the margarine into the flour, using a coarse grater. Mix the margarine flakes lightly through the flour to give an evenly rough consistency, without actually rubbing the margarine into the flour. Mix the pastry with just enough water to make a firm dough; it should be just a little softer than the consistency of shortcrust pastry. Wrap the pastry in greaseproof paper and leave it in a cold place overnight.

Roll the pastry into a rectangle about 12 x 10 inches (30 x 25.5 cm) and trim it to shape. Keep the scraps for the decoration. Lift the pastry on the rolling pin onto an upturned baking tray then place the cod steaks along the centre, almost touching.

Beat the butter and add the chopped parsley, salt and pepper and a squeeze of lemon juice. Spread this mixture over the fish. Brush around the edges with water and close the pastry first down the centre then at the ends. Press the joins well together and flute them down the centre. Brush the surface with egg glaze. Make some leaves with the pastry scraps and put them on the top; brush these with egg.

Bake the fish slice in a hot oven, at about gas mark 7 (425 °F, 220 °C) for 20 minutes then turn the heat down to gas mark 5 (375 °F, 190 °C) for a further 10 minutes. Cut the slice into four large pieces, and serve with new potatoes sprinkled with parsley.

Mary Meredith

Quenelles of Fish with Lemon Sauce

(Serves 4)

Coley is a fish often spurned at the fishmongers because of its colour; yet the slight greyishness disappears during cooking, leaving it as white as cod. For pies, mousselines and other fish mixtures, coley is cheap, tasty and delicious.

1½ lb fresh coley (700 g)
a few fish bones
1 small onion
1 bay leaf
a few peppercorns
salt and pepper
1 sprig of thyme
3 large egg whites
½ pint double cream (275 ml)
1 oz butter (25 g)
1 oz plain flour (25 g)
2 large eggs
1 large lemon

Remove the skin and bones from the coley and put them with the rinsed fish bones in a large pan. Cover them with cold water. Skin the onion and add it to the pan with the bay leaf, peppercorns, and a pinch of salt and the thyme. Bring to the boil and simmer for 15 minutes.

Meanwhile, mince the fish twice and put it in a bowl. Whisk the egg whites fairly stiffly and gradually work them into the fish. Lightly whip the cream and whisk this into the fish mixture and lastly season it well with salt and pepper. Bring a large pan of salted water to the boil and taking up the fish mixture in tablespoons, gently poach a few at a time for 5–10 minutes or until they are puffed and cooked. Drain them well and keep hot.

While they cook, melt the butter in a pan and stir in the flour and cook this roux gently for 1 minute. Strain the fish stock and measure ½ pint (275 ml). Gradually stir this into the roux then bring to the boil and simmer it for 2 minutes. Season the sauce well with salt and pepper. Whisk the eggs until they are light and frothy. Squeeze out and strain the juice from the lemon and whisk it into the eggs with 2 tablespoons cold water. Whisk in half the sauce, a tablespoon at a time, then return the mixture to the sauce in the pan and heat it gently, stirring all the time. Don't let it boil because it will curdle. Serve the quenelles with the lemon sauce poured over them.

Kathie Webber

Very Fishy Stew (Serves 4)

Soups are one of the most comforting of all foods—and they are blissfully cheap and easy to make. This one is very substantial, really a cross between a soup and a stew, nicely combining first and main course in one dish. I serve aioli with it and a selection of breads. A crisp salad and cheese—eaten together in the French fashion—go well afterwards, and/or a fresh lemon sorbet.

2 large mackerel, filleted
½ lb coley fillets (225 g)
plenty of extra fish bones and trimmings
¾ lb potatoes (350 g)
3 large leeks
6 celery stalks
14 oz can tomatoes (400 g)
¼ pint white wine or dry cider
2 tablespoons butter
salt, pepper
1 bay leaf, a few parsley stalks
½ teaspoon dried marjoram

Put the fish bones and trimmings into a pan together with bay, parsley, 1 pint water (570 ml) and the liquid from the canned tomatoes. Bring to the boil, skim, cover and simmer for 20 minutes. Strain through muslin, reserving the liquid. Slice the potatoes, leeks and celery and sweat in butter in a covered pan for a few minutes. Shake the pan occasionally to prevent sticking. Add the fish stock, season well with salt and pepper, cover and simmer until the vegetables are just tender. Add the tomatoes, marjoram and wine and bring back to boiling point. Add the coley cut into 2 inch cubes (5 cm) and the mackerel fillets cut into thick slices. Cover and simmer for 10 minutes. Check seasoning before serving.

Philippa Davenport

Casserole of Fish with Ginger and Onion (Serves 6–8)

1 or more fish (about 2–2½ lb), sea-bass, mackerel, large herrings, etcetera (about 1 kg)
3 large onions
8 slices of root ginger
vegetable oil for deep frying
½ pint good stock (275 ml)
½ a chicken stock cube
4 tablespoons soya sauce
4 tablespoons sherry
2 teaspoons sugar
3 tablespoons vinegar

Clean the fish thoroughly, and pat to dry. Cut onions into thin slices, and ginger into shreds.

Heat the oil in a deep saucepan. When hot (when a crumb dropped in will sizzle) lower the fish to deep fry for 6-7 minutes. Remove and drain. Heat 3 tablespoons oil in a flameproof casserole. Add onion and ginger and stir-fry them over medium heat for 4–5 minutes. Pour in the stock, add the stock cube, soya sauce, sherry and sugar. When the contents start to boil, allow them to simmer for 5 minutes. Add the fish, or pieces of fish, and bury them under the onion and ginger and baste them with the sauce. Place a lid firmly on the casserole and put it in a pre-heated oven at gas mark 6 (400 °F, 200 °C). Leave to cook for 40 minutes. Turn the fish over and cook for a further 30 minutes.

Serve by bringing the casserole to the table. Because of the lengthy cooking, at least some of the bones of the fish should be edible. Still another excellent dish to consume with rice, or with the Vegetarian Fried Rice on page 154.

West Coast Fish Stew

(Serves 4)

Check the prices in your fishmongers and choose an inexpensive fish for this dish, pollock, coley or grey mullet, etcetera. Although very similar to a French Bouillabaisse, this kind of fish stew also used to be very popular with fishing families in the West of England.

1½ lbs fresh cod fillet, coley or pollock, etcetera (700 g)
flour
cayenne pepper
2 sticks celery
1 onion
2 leeks
2 carrots
2 cloves garlic
6 small ripe tomatoes
1 tablespoon tomato purée
2 anchovy fillets
1 teaspoon capers
2 bay leaves
a pinch each of thyme and sage
1½ pints chicken or fish stock (850 ml)
4 tablespoons olive oil
salt and freshly ground black pepper
a pinch of saffron soaked in 1 tablespoon boiling water

Cut the fish into pieces roughly 2 inches square (5 cm). Roll the fish pieces in flour seasoned with salt and a little cayenne pepper. Heat the oil in a saucepan until smoking. Add the fish and cook quickly over a high heat until the fish is crisp and golden brown on both sides. Remove from the pan and drain off excess fat on kitchen paper. Leave the fish on one side. Strain remaining oil into a saucepan.

Peel and thinly slice the celery and onion. Clean and thinly slice the leeks. Peel and thinly slice the carrots. Peel and crush the garlic cloves. Peel tomatoes, remove cores and roughly chop the flesh.

69

Heat the oil in the saucepan, add celery, onion, leeks, garlic and carrots and cook over a low heat until the onions are soft and transparent. Add tomatoes, tomato purée, anchovies (roughly chopped), the capers and herbs (except saffron) and mix well. Add the stock, season with salt and pepper and bring to the boil. Cover and simmer gently for 5 minutes. Strain off the saffron juice and add to the stew for the last 5 minutes of cooking time.

Place the fried fish in the bottom of a large heated serving dish. Pour over the very hot stew and serve at once.

Marika Hanbury Tenison

Smoked Haddock Lasagne (Serves 4)

Smoked cod or coley make a satisfactory and slightly cheaper version of this.

6 oz lasagne (175 g)
salt and oil for cooking
1 lb smoked haddock (450 g)
1 pint milk (570 ml)
1 bay leaf
2 oz butter (50 g)
2 oz flour (50 g)
5 oz grated cheese (150 g)

Boil the lasagne in 5 pints of water (3 litres), slightly salted and containing a tablespoon of oil. Cook for 15–17 minutes, drain at once and return to the saucepan, stirring in a dessertspoon of melted butter or oil.

Meanwhile poach the haddock in the milk with the bay leaf. Remove the fish and cool. Make a roux with the butter and flour, and strain in the cooking milk, stirring to make a smooth sauce. Beat 4 oz of the cheese (110 g) into the sauce. Skin, bone and flake the fish.

Put a layer of lasagne into a well-buttered ovenproof dish, then a layer of flaked fish and one of sauce. Repeat, finishing again with the sauce, sprinkle with more grated cheese and bake at gas mark 6 (400 °F, 200 °C) until golden brown.

Harold Wilshaw.

Smoked Haddock Soufflé (Serves 2–4)

8 oz smoked haddock, cooked, skinned and flaked (225 g)
½ oz butter (10 g)
¼ oz flour (5 g)
¼ pint milk (150 ml)
1 oz grated cheese (25 g)
1 teaspoon lemon juice
1 teaspoon chopped parsley
pepper and cayenne
3 eggs

Melt the butter, stir in the flour and gradually add the milk to make a thick sauce. Stir in the fish, and for a really creamy soufflé, press through a coarse sieve or put through a food mill.

Stir in the cheese, lemon juice, parsley and seasonings and the well-beaten egg yolks. Cool and fold in the stiffly beaten egg whites—add an extra white if you have one to spare—and bake in the middle of a moderate oven, gas mark 4 (350 °F, 180 °C) for 30 minutes.

Margaret Costa.

Creamed Finnan Haddie (Serves 6)

2 lb smoked haddock (900 g)
water and milk, to cover
3 tablespoons butter
3 tablespoons flour
¾ pint cream (425 ml)
freshly ground black pepper and nutmeg
triangles of bread
butter

Soak the haddock in water for 2 hours. Drain, place in a saucepan and cover with equal amounts of water and milk and bring to a fast boil. Remove from the heat and allow to stand for 15 minutes, then drain, reserving the stock.

Melt 3 tablespoons of butter in the top of a double saucepan; stir in the flour and cook over direct heat for 3 minutes, stirring continuously until smooth. Place the top of the double saucepan over hot water, add the cream and ½ pint of haddock stock (275 ml) and continue to cook, stirring from time to time. Season to taste with freshly ground black pepper and a little grated nutmeg.

Remove the skin and bones from the haddock and break into pieces. Fold pieces into sauce and simmer gently until ready to serve. Serve in a shallow casserole with triangles of bread which you have sautéed in butter.

Kippery Kedgeree

(Serves 4)

If you hanker after one of those grand Victorian breakfasts one morning, you could make a start with a nice buttery kedgeree, made here with kippers instead of the more usual smoked haddock. It makes an equally nice, and easy, lunch dish.

approximately 1 lb kippers (2 pairs) (450 g)
2 tablespoons butter
1 onion, chopped
1 tea cup long grain rice
4 oz mushrooms, cut in wedges (110 g)
1 oz extra butter (25 g)
1 teaspoon lemon juice
¼ teaspoon hot curry powder
3 hardboiled eggs, chopped
chopped parsley to garnish

First of all pour a good pint of boiling water over the kippers in a pan, then leave them on one side for 5 minutes. After that drain them—reserving the water—and flake the fish into chunks, discarding the skin, head and bones. The reserved water should be strained into a jug and kept on one side till needed.

Now heat the 2 tablespoons of butter in a saucepan and fry the onion for 5 minutes before stirring in the rice and curry powder. Stir the rice around so it gets a good coating of butter, then add two cupfuls of the reserved water. Bring to simmering point and cook (covered) over a low heat until all the liquid has been absorbed and the rice is tender.

Meanwhile in a separate saucepan melt the remaining butter, add the lemon juice and cook the mushrooms in it until they are tender (about 3 minutes). Then add the contents of this pan to the cooked rice, along with the flaked kipper and one of the hardboiled eggs (chopped first). Blend everything together gently with a fork, then taste and season as required with salt and freshly milled pepper. Serve immediately in a warmed serving dish, with the remaining chopped hardboiled eggs, a sprinkling of parsley and a knob of butter on top.

Baked Mackerel with Lemon (Serves 4)

Simple to prepare, this is Rosemary Hume's own way of serving freshly caught mackerel in Scotland.

4 mackerel
2 large onions
1 lemon
1 large spray parsley
¾ oz butter (15 g)
salt and pepper from the mill
2 fl oz wine vinegar (50 ml)
6 fl oz cider (170 ml)
1 tablespoon brown crumbs

Fillet the mackerel. Slice the onions finely, cover with cold water and bring to the boil; strain and refresh with cold water and drain well. Remove the peel and pith from the lemon with a serrated edged knife and cut in thin slices. Strip the leaves from the parsley and mix them with the onion and lemon.

Butter the bottom of a fireproof dish, put half the onion mixture on this and arrange the mackerel fillets on top. Scatter over the remainder of the onion mixture and season well with salt and freshly ground black pepper.

Mix together the vinegar and cider and pour over the fish.

Sprinkle the brown crumbs over the top and dot with tiny shavings of butter.

Bake in a slow oven at gas mark 3 (325 °F, 170 °C) for about 40 minutes. Serve cold with brown bread and butter.

Rosemary Hume

Muriel Downes

Soused Mackerel (Serves 4)

One of our great British fish, herrings have almost disappeared from the fishmonger's slab, one hopes only temporarily. But we don't have to ignore all the recipes which were associated with herrings. Mackerel make a very good substitute, particularly in this dish.

4 mackerel
1 onion
salt and pepper
2 small bay leaves
malt vinegar
water
1 level tablespoon mixed pickling spice

Cut the heads off the mackerel and trim fins and tails. Slit underside and clean. Lay fish skin uppermost on a board and press down centre back to loosen backbone. Turn over and remove backbone. Peel and finely chop onion. Sprinkle each mackerel with salt, pepper and chopped onion. Roll up from head end around ½ a bayleaf. Place in an ovenproof dish. Mix equal quantities of vinegar and water together and pour over mackerel to cover. Sprinkle with pickling spice, cover dish and cook in a moderate oven at gas mark 4 (350 °F, 180 °C) for about 1 hour or until fish is cooked. Remove from oven and leave to cool in dish. Serve cold with salad for a light lunch or supper dish.

Frances M. Walcott

South African Pickled Fish (Serves 3)

This is a curious mixture of Western and Eastern traditions. Pickling pieces of fish in vinegar is common in many European countries; this combined with the spices of Indian cookery produces an outstanding dish.

It is best to use firm-textured fish with a strong flavour for this dish: cod and haddock are obvious examples, but rock salmon, coley (saithe) and monkfish are also very good. However, in my experience the finest flavour of all comes from grey mullet.

1 lb white fish (450 g)
2 large onions
½ pint malt vinegar (300 ml)
1 tablespoon curry powder
1 teaspoon cayenne pepper (vary the amount if necessary)
1 tablespoon white sugar
salt, black pepper
flour

Divide the fish into large pieces, making sure that you have removed all the bones, and rub with salt and black pepper. Leave for an hour. Then coat the fish lightly in flour and fry in oil, but don't overcook it. Lift out the pieces and let them drain well. Peel off the skin before putting them into a shallow dish.

Meanwhile slice the onions and put into a saucepan with the vinegar, sugar and spices. (It is best to mix the powders with a little vinegar before adding them to the saucepan.) Bring to the boil, stirring well, and simmer for 10 minutes. Finally pour the hot pickle over the fish, making sure that it is covered. Leave the dish in a cool place for 24 hours before using.

The fish is eaten cold with plenty of bread to soak up the liquid; the whole mixture is eaten, and plates should be covered with fish, onions and pickle. Part of the attraction of this is the contrast between the soft fish and the crisp onion pieces. Think of it rather as a cold curry, where the sauce is an essential part of the whole dish.

In South Africa I am told this dish is eaten on Good Friday morning with hot cross buns!

David Mabey

Meat, Poultry and Game

Tickler's Pie

(Serves 4)

This is my interpretation of a recipe I was told about by an old codger who used to make most of his money by 'tickling' the salmon from other people's rivers. His granny, he said, knew how to make a 'real' pie from the ends of a joint, a pie that had a 'bite' to it. (Tickling, by the way, is the art of catching salmon and trout in the hand by stroking them into a comatose state.)

1 lb cooked beef (450 g)
2 onions
1 heaped tablespoon meat dripping
1 tablespoon flour
½ tablespoon curry powder
2 tablespoons tomato chutney
1 pint stock (570 ml)
1½ lb potatoes (700 g)
½ oz butter (10 g)
½ teaspoon made English mustard
2 oz grated Cheddar cheese
salt and pepper

Coarsely mince the beef. Peel and very thinly slice the onions. Peel the potatoes and boil them until tender. Drain well and mash with the butter, mustard and half the cheese. Season the mashed potatoes with salt and pepper.

Melt the dripping in a large frying pan and add the onions. Cook over a low heat until the onions are soft and transparent. Add the meat, sprinkle over the flour and curry powder and mix well. Cook, stirring continually for 2 minutes and then gradually mix in the stock. Bring to the boil, cover and simmer for 20 minutes. Add the chutney, season with salt and pepper if necessary and cook for a further 20 minutes.

Transfer the meat to a baking dish, spoon off any excess stock and spread the potatoes on top of the meat. Sprinkle over the remaining cheese and bake in a hot oven, gas mark 7 (425 °F, 220 °C) for 15-20 minutes until the top is a delicious golden brown.

Marika Hanbury Tenison

81

Special Easy Lasagne (Serves 6)

For the meat sauce:
1 tablespoon oil
1 lb raw minced beef (450 g)
1 oz streaky bacon, de-rinded and chopped (25 g)
8 oz onions, chopped (225 g)
4 sticks celery, chopped
½ oz flour (10 g)
½ pint water (275 ml)
3½ oz can tomato purée (90 g)
2 cloves garlic, crushed
2 teaspoons redcurrant jelly
1 beef stock cube
½ teaspoon salt
pepper
¼ teaspoon dried herbs

For the white sauce:
1½ oz butter (35 g)
1½ oz flour (35 g)
½ teaspoon made mustard
¼ teaspoon nutmeg
salt and pepper
1 pint milk (570 ml)

4 oz Cheddar cheese, grated
4 oz Emmenthal cheese, grated
½ oz Parmesan cheese, grated

5 oz uncooked lasagne (Barilla pasta gives you 9 pieces)

For the meat sauce: heat the oil in a pan, add the beef and bacon and fry until browned. Add the onions and celery and cook for 5 minutes, stir in the flour and then the remaining sauce ingredients, stir well and bring to the boil, cover and simmer for 1 hour, stirring from time to time.

For the white sauce: melt the butter in a large pan and stir in the flour, mustard, nutmeg, salt and pepper and cook gently for 2 minutes. Remove the pan from the heat and gradually add the milk, stirring to make a smooth mixture. Return the pan to the heat and cook, stirring until the sauce has thickened.

Combine the Cheddar and Emmenthal cheese.

If you are going to freeze the lasagne, use a foil dish 9 x 9 inches (23 x 23 cm) or a 3½ pint (2 litre) shallow casserole lined with foil. In the dish put ¼ of the meat sauce, ¼ of the white sauce and ¼ of the mixed cheese, followed by ⅓ of the uncooked lasagne (lay edge to edge, not overlapping) which is usually 3 pieces. If necessary break the lasagne to size. Then start again with ¼ of the meat sauce, white sauce and mixed cheeses and ⅓ of the lasagne. Repeat, finishing with a final layer of meat sauce, white sauce and cheese and the grated Parmesan cheese.

To serve at once, leave until cold and then cook at gas mark 4 (350 °F, 180 °C) for about 45 minutes to 1 hour or until the top is brown and bubbling.

To freeze, cool the lasagne and if using a foil tray, cover, seal and label. If using a foil-lined casserole, remove the lasagne when solid, overwrap, seal, label and use within one month. To serve from the freezer, remove all wrappings from foil-wrapped lasagne, return to casserole and thaw overnight in the refrigerator. If the lasagne is in a foil dish, uncover and thaw similarly. Cook as above.

Mary Berry.

Chilli con Carne

(Serves 4)

The following recipe is a very free adaptation of the famous Mexican dish. It is economical, full of flavour and easy to make. It is an ideal meal for preparing in advance, if for example you are going to be out all day. It just needs to be reheated and doesn't need any extra carbohydrate, such as rice or potatoes, unless you particularly want it.

olive or other vegetable oil
2 large onions
1 green pepper (optional)
1 lb tomatoes or 1 x 15 oz can tomatoes (450 g)
1 tablespoon tomato paste
1 lb minced beef (450 g)
2½ oz pack dried soya mince (soaked in a little water) (60 g)
3 teaspoons bruised cumin seed (the bruising is essential to release flavour)
½ teaspoon cayenne pepper (or more if you like it hot)
1 teaspoon brown sugar
1 teaspoon salt
1 glass red wine or 2 tablespoons vinegar
1 lb red kidney beans or haricot beans, soaked overnight (450 g) (or a can of baked beans as a last resort)
enough water to make a thick stew (use liquid from the beans)

Heat the oil in a large saucepan. Slice onions and green pepper and stew in oil until slightly tender. Add tomatoes (peeled and chopped), tomato paste, mince and soya granules. Stir very thoroughly. Add cumin seed, cayenne, sugar, salt, wine or vinegar and blend well together. Add the beans and enough liquid to make a thick consistency. Cook gently for about 1½ hours, or until the beans are tender. (The beans may be precooked in a pressure cooker to save time.) Serve in earthenware bowls with crusty bread and green salad.

Anna Macmiaidhachain

Spicy Meatballs

(Serves 3–4)

I'm a great fan of pressure cooking as it does save so much time and fuel, but for those who do not possess one you will find I have included in the recipe how to cook the dish in the oven.

1 lb minced raw beef (450 g)
1 medium onion, peeled and finely chopped
1 level tablespoon tomato ketchup
a little Worcestershire sauce
salt and pepper
2 level tablespoons dry white breadcrumbs
1 large egg
½ pint beef stock (275 ml)
1½ lb potatoes, peeled and cubed (700 g)
1 level teaspoon allspice berries
1 level teaspoon paprika pepper

Put the minced beef into a bowl, add the onion, tomato ketchup, Worcestershire sauce, seasoning and breadcrumbs and when the ingredients are well mixed bind them together with the egg. Divide the mixture into 8 and roll each piece into a ball.

Bring the stock to the boil in the pressure cooker and drop in the meatballs. Add the prepared potatoes and gently stir them into the stock, then sprinkle over the allspice berries, paprika pepper and a little seasoning. Cover the cooker and following the manufacturers' instructions bring it to high pressure (15 lb). Maintain this pressure for 10 minutes.

Reduce the pressure under cold running water then open the cooker and carefully lift out the meatballs. Turn the potatoes and stock into a serving dish, arrange the meatballs on top and complete the meal with a green or tomato salad.

Note: To cook this recipe in the oven, arrange the meatballs and potatoes in a shallow ovenproof dish, pour over the boiling stock and sprinkle with allspice berries, paprika pepper and seasoning. Bake the dish in the centre of a moderate oven, gas mark 4 (350 °F, 180 °C) for about 1 hour or until the meatballs are brown and the potatoes tender.

Janet Warren

Terbiyeli Köfte (Serves 4)

This meatball stew in a tasty egg and lemon sauce is a Turkish peasant dish. It's very useful for family meals.

1 lb minced beef or veal (450 g)
4 oz rice (110 g)
a handful of parsley
1 onion
2 dessertspoons flour
1 egg
juice of 2 lemons
1 teaspoon paprika
1 oz butter (25 g)
salt, black pepper

If possible, ask the butcher to mince the meat twice. Chop the onion and parsley very finely and mix with the minced meat. Stir in the rice, salt and plenty of black pepper. Form into small balls the size of a marble. This is easier to do with wet hands. Bring 1¾ pints (1 litre) of salted water to the boil in a large pan. Drop in the meatballs and when they have come to the boil again remove scum. Simmer gently for ½ hour. In a small saucepan whisk the egg, lemon juice, a coffee cup full of water and the flour. Bring to the boil slowly, stirring all the time. If it seems to thicken too much add a little water. Stir the mixture gradually into the meatballs and water. Before serving melt the butter with a teaspoon of paprika and trickle on the top.

Josceline Dimbleby

Meatballs with Peppers and Tomatoes (Serves 4)

My search for the perfect meatball has taken many years. Of course the quality of the meat you use is all-important, but I think this recipe is the best yet discovered.

1 lb best-quality ground beef (450 g)
½ lb good pork sausagemeat (225 g)
½ a green pepper, finely chopped
1 egg, beaten
1 medium onion, minced or very finely chopped
1 large clove garlic, crushed
¾ level teaspoon dried mixed herbs
1 tablespoon fresh chopped parsley
2 slices of bread
2 tablespoons milk
1 dessertspoon tomato purée
flour, for coating
oil, for frying
salt and freshly milled black pepper

For the sauce:
14 oz tin Italian tomatoes (400 g)
or 1 lb ripe tomatoes, peeled and chopped (450 g)
1 small onion, chopped
1 clove garlic, crushed
½ a green pepper, chopped
1 level teaspoon dried basil

Begin by cutting the crusts off the bread and soaking it in the milk. Then mash it to crumbs with a fork and, in a large mixing bowl, mix it together with the rest of the meatball ingredients and salt and pepper very thoroughly with your hands. Now take pieces of the mixture—about a tablespoonful—and roll them into small rounds. You should get about 16–18 altogether.

Coat each one lightly with flour then, in a large frying pan, brown them in the oil. Meanwhile pre-heat the oven to gas mark 5 (375 °F, 190 °C). When the meatballs are browned, transfer them to a casserole, and in the juices remaining in the pan soften the onion and green pepper for 5 minutes before adding the tomatoes, garlic and basil, then simmer for a couple of minutes. Taste and season, then pour the sauce over the meatballs in the casserole and cook, with a lid, in the oven for 45 minutes. After that take the lid off and cook for a further 15–20 minutes. This is nice served on a bed of buttered noodles with a crisp green salad.

Beef with Green Peas (Serves 4)

This is best with peas from the garden but can be made with frozen. The peas go to mush but it is so good that nobody cares.

a piece of topside of beef, about 2 lb (900 g)
4 oz butter (110 g)
salt and pepper
2 pints peas (1.15 litres)

Seal the beef in a frying pan in the butter. Season it with salt and pepper and transfer it to a casserole which just takes it with about ½ inch (1 cm) all round. Fill this with the peas, pour over the butter from the frying pan, cover tightly and cook in the oven at gas mark 1 (275 °F, 140 °C) for 2–2½ hours.

Harold Wilshaw.

Pot Roast
(Serves 8)

The secret of this pot roast is that *at no time* do you add water. The fat and juices from the meat and juices from the vegetables supply plenty of liquid.

4 lb rolled brisket (2 kg)
2 large or 4 small onions, chopped fine
3 fresh tomatoes, chopped
pepper and salt

Pre-heat the oven to gas mark 4 (350 °F, 180 °C).

Wipe the meat thoroughly and place in a very hot iron casserole. Turn frequently over the heat so that the meat becomes dark brown on all sides. Place in a moderate oven for 2 hours or until it begins to get tender. Then season with salt and pepper. It will require quite a bit of salt which will cook into the meat. Put back into the oven for another ½ hour, then add the onions and tomatoes. Cook for another four hours until the meat is really tender and the vegetables have been reduced to a dark brown pulp. When the meat is thoroughly tender remove it from the pot. Then remove as much fat as possible from the gravy which includes the vegetables. Again *do not add any water* to gravy. Serve.

Rosalinda Harlock

Barbecued Pork Slices

(Serves 4)

This is a very economical supper dish, using my own variation of a barbecue sauce which comes out of the oven rich, piquant and caramelised!

4–6 pork slices
1 small onion, finely chopped
4 tablespoons dry cider
6 tablespoons soya sauce
1 tablespoon tomato purée
1 teaspoon English mustard
1 clove garlic
1 level tablespoon soft brown sugar
freshly milled pepper

Pre-heat the oven to gas mark 6 (400 °F, 200 °C).

First of all arrange the pork slices side by side in a roasting tin, then pop the chopped onion in between them. Now half-cook the meat in the oven—about half an hour. Meanwhile make up the barbecue sauce, simply by crushing the garlic clove and mixing it in a bowl with the rest of the ingredients. When the cooking time for the pork is up, pour off any excess fat from the tin, then pour in the barbecue sauce all over the meat and cook for a further 20–25 minutes, basting frequently.

Barbecued Spare Ribs   (Serves 5–6)

4 lb spare ribs (the rib cage of pork) (2 kg)
2 medium onions
6 slices root ginger (optional)
6 tablespoons soya sauce
3 tablespoons vegetable oil
2 tablespoons hoisin sauce (optional)
3 teaspoons sugar
½ pint good stock (275 ml)
1 chicken stock cube
pepper (to taste)
1 tablespoon cornflour, blended in 5–6 tablespoons water
1 tablespoon sherry

Cut the spare ribs into individual ribs. Parboil them for 5 minutes and drain. Cut onion into thin slices and shred ginger.

Heat the oil in a flameproof casserole. Add onion and ginger. Stir them around in the hot oil for 2 minutes. Add the ribs, sprinkle them with half the soya sauce. Continue to stir them around with the other ingredients over a high heat for 3 minutes. Add hoisin sauce, stock, stock cube, sugar, pepper and the remaining soya sauce. Bring the contents to the boil and insert the casserole into a pre-heated oven at gas mark 6 (400 °F, 200 °C). Leave to cook for ¾ hour.

Remove the ribs from the casserole and spread them out on a roasting pan. Insert the pan into the oven at gas mark 7 (425 °F, 220 °C) for 7–8 minutes for the ribs to crisp.

Meanwhile place the casserole over a medium heat on the cooker and add the blended cornflour and sherry. Stir until the sauce thickens. Pour the sauce into a bowl or sauceboat.

Serve the ribs on a well-heated dish (there should be about 20 pieces of them) for the diners to pick up and eat with their fingers. The sauce can be poured over the ribs, or used as a dip for those who prefer to eat spareribs with sauce. We in China usually eat them with 'steamed bread', but they should be just as good with ordinary slices of toast.

Coarse Pork Pâté (Serves 8–10)

Two inexpensive ingredients combine here to make an excellent pâté which combines well with ham or other sliced delicatessen meats to make a cold platter for buffets or lunches.

1 lb pigs' liver (450 g)
2 lb belly of pork (900 g)
1 slice day old white bread with crusts removed
1 oz butter (25 g)
1 large onion
1 egg
2 level teaspoons salt
freshly milled pepper
1 teaspoon dried mixed herbs
2 tablespoons dry sherry
½ lb streaky bacon rashers (225 g)
2 bay leaves

Trim and cut the liver into pieces. Remove any rib bones and rind from the belly of pork—your butcher will do this for you. Cut the pork in pieces. Pass the liver and pork belly through the coarse blade of a mincer once or twice according to the texture you like. Then pass the slice of bread, broken in pieces, through the mincer last of all to push through the last few pieces of pork and liver. Melt the butter in a saucepan and add the peeled and finely chopped onion. Cover and fry gently until the onion is soft, but not brown. Add the softened onion and butter from the pan, the egg, salt and a good seasoning of pepper, the mixed herbs and the sherry to the pork mixture. Mix very thoroughly with a wooden spoon. Trim the rind from the bacon rashers and then flatten each one by pressing along the work surface with a knife. Use all but two or three rashers to line a large 9 x 5 x 3 inch loaf tin (23 x 13 x 7.5 cm) or an oblong pâté dish. Spoon in the pâté mixture and cover with the remaining bacon rashers. Top with the bay leaves. Cover with foil or a lid and set the dish in a larger roasting tin with about 1 inch cold water (2.5 cm). Set in a slow oven, gas mark 3 (325 °F, 170 °C) and cook for 2¼ hours. Cool, then leave overnight under a weight. Turn out and serve sliced.

Katie Stewart.

Forehock of Bacon (Roast or Boiled)

This forequarter joint weighs about 7 or 8 lb (3–3.5 kg) before it is boned; if you want to cook it with the bone in then calculate the time with this weight. We found on boning the joint that it weighed about 5 lb (2.25 kg) so we calculated the time accordingly, allowing 25 minutes per pound (450 g). To bone the forehock, cut the rib bones from the underside and slit the joint through the skin, down to the bone on the underside, to expose the bone. Cut the meat as close to the bone as possible then remove it.

a forehock of bacon, smoked or unsmoked
2 level tablespoons demerara sugar
2 sprigs of rosemary, if available
browned breadcrumbs

Bone the meat and sprinkle the inside with demerara sugar, then close it up neatly and tie it into shape with string.

To roast the joint: lay a large piece of kitchen foil on the work surface. This should be big enough to wrap the forehock completely; you may have to pleat the edges of 2 pieces together. Put the joint in the centre, with the sprigs of rosemary on top, and wrap it like parcel, turning the ends upwards. Lift it into a roasting tin and put it into the centre of the oven at gas mark 5 (375 °F, 190 °C), to cook for the calculated time.

To boil the joint: put the joint into the pan, cover it with cold water, add the sprigs of rosemary and bring it slowly to the boil, starting the cooking time at the moment the water boils. Simmer gently for the calculated period. Leave the joint in the water until it is cool enough to handle.

Unwrap the joint if it has been roasted or lift it out of the pan if it has been boiled; do this on the draining board as there will be a certain amount of juice. Remove the outer skin, which should peel off quite easily with a little help from the knife. Dust the fat surface well with the browned crumbs before serving, either hot or cold.

Any scraps which remain can be used for omelettes, quiche lorraine, a pâté or simply sliced and fried with eggs. The really fatty end piece is excellent sliced thinly and used to cover a chicken while it is roasting in the oven.

Mary Berenith

Bacon and Corned Beef Loaf (Serves 6)

When you have some left-over boiled bacon in the house, use it to make a particularly savoury meat loaf. You can bake it in a loaf tin in the usual way or pack it into one or two round tins—a cocoa tin, for instance—well greased and lightly sprinkled with fine crumbs. This will give you attractive round slices when the loaf is cut.

1 lb left-over boiled bacon (450 g)
6–8 oz corned beef (175–225 g)
4 oz fresh crumbs (110 g)
2 tablespoons finely chopped onion
1 tablespoon finely chopped parsley
1 tablespoon ketchup or chutney
1 teaspoon grated lemon rind
salt and pepper
1 egg
2½ fl oz milk (70 ml)

Put both bacon and corned beef through the mincer, using a fine cutter. Blend with the other ingredients and season well. Grease a loaf-shaped tin, pack the mixture into it and bake in a moderate oven, gas mark 4 (350 °F, 180 °C) for about 1¼ hours. Less time is needed if two smaller tins are used.

This can be served hot or cold and is delicious with salad. To make an interesting texture mince the bacon only and add the corned beef chopped finely. Cooked veal can be used instead of corned beef.

Margaret Costa

Lamb in Dill Sauce (Serves 6)

Classically, this very refined dish is made with the best cuts of lamb. But it works beautifully with any cut, though naturally the simmering time will be longer for cheaper cuts.

2 lb lean leg of lamb, cut into large chunks (900 g)
1 onion, sliced
1 carrot, sliced
1 dessertspoon crushed dill seeds, or 3–4 sprigs of fresh dill
1 bay leaf
12 peppercorns
1 chicken stock cube
1 tablespoon flour
1 oz butter (25 g)
1 dessertspoon lemon juice
1 egg yolk
3 tablespoons double cream

Put the meat, onion, carrot, stalks (or seeds) of dill (but not the fresh leaves), bay leaf, peppercorns and stock cube into a saucepan. Cover with water and bring slowly to the boil. Turn down the heat and cook as slowly as possible for 1 hour if using meat from the leg or best end, longer for cheaper cuts—anything up to 2 hours. Lift out the cubes of meat, and put them into a casserole or serving dish. Cover to prevent drying out.

Strain the stock, and skim off all the fat. An easy way to do this is to lay successive sheets of absorbent kitchen paper, or paper napkins, on the top of the liquid—they will soak up the fat. When quite fat-free, measure the remaining liquid, and return to the saucepan. You need ¾ pint (425 ml). If you haven't enough, make it up with water. If it is too much, boil it rapidly until reduced. Mix the butter and flour together on a plate until you have a smooth paste. Whisk this into the hot stock, and whisk steadily until the sauce is smooth. Bring to the boil and simmer for 2 minutes. If the meat is to be kept until tomorrow, pour the sauce over the meat and cool. Refrigerate once cold.

Reheat the lamb and sauce in a heavy saucepan. Once hot proceed as follows. Mix the egg yolk and cream in a bowl. Pour a little of the hot sauce on to the cream mixture, and then stir this back into the stew. Be very careful not to boil the sauce now or the yolk will scramble. Flavour the sauce with the lemon juice and add more salt and pepper if necessary. Chop the dill leaves if you have them, and stir them into the sauce just before serving. Tip into a serving bowl, and serve with mashed potatoes.

Prudence Leith.

Lamb Hash Parmentier (Serves 4)

1 lb cooked lamb, diced (450 g)
6 medium potatoes
4 level tablespoons butter
1 egg, well beaten
salt and freshly ground black pepper
butter and olive oil, for frying
1 Spanish onion, finely chopped
½ pint well-flavoured tomato sauce, or thickened tomato-flavoured
    lamb gravy (275 ml)
3–4 level tablespoons freshly grated Parmesan cheese

97

Peel and boil the potatoes. Mash 4 of them with butter and well-beaten egg; season to taste with salt and freshly ground black pepper and force through a piping bag to make a border around a shallow ovenproof dish.

Dice the remaining 2 potatoes and fry in equal quantities of butter and olive oil until golden. Drain and reserve.

Fry the finely chopped onion in 2 tablespoons olive oil until transparent. Add the diced lamb and continue to cook until both onion and lamb begin to turn golden. Season generously with salt and freshly ground black pepper. Stir in the fried potatoes; pour over the tomato sauce or gravy and simmer gently for 10 to 15 minutes, stirring from time to time. Correct seasoning.

Spoon the hash into the centre of the potato border; sprinkle with freshly grated Parmesan and cook in a hot oven, gas mark 8 (450 °F, 230 °C) for 10 to 12 minutes, or until golden brown.

Turkish Stuffed Peppers (Serves 4)

No one can afford to waste a scrap of meat nowadays. Here's an excellent way to use up any leftover lamb—in fact it's almost worth buying a bigger joint for.

4 medium sized green or red peppers
¾ lb (approximately) cooked lamb, cut up into very small pieces (350 g)
2 medium onions, peeled and chopped
2 cloves garlic, chopped small
14 oz tin Italian tomatoes (400 g)
or 1 lb ripe tomatoes, peeled and chopped (450 g)
4 teaspoons tomato purée
2 level tablespoons currants
½ teaspoon ground cinnamon
½ teaspoon marjoram
2 dessertspoons pinenuts (if available—most health food shops stock them)
1 large tea cup long-grain rice
2½ tea cups boiling water
dripping
salt and freshly milled pepper

Pre-heat the oven to gas mark 5 (375 °F, 190 °C).

Begin by melting some (lamb) dripping in a saucepan, then stir in the rice. When it has absorbed all the fat pour in 2½ cups of boiling water, and add a sprinkling of salt. Put a lid on and simmer for approximately 25 minutes, or until all the liquid has been absorbed.

Meanwhile fry the onions and garlic in a little more dripping for a couple of minutes, then add the meat together with the currants and pinenuts. Season well with salt and pepper, stir in the spices and two of the tomatoes plus a tablespoon of juice from the contents of the tin, then turn the heat very low and leave to simmer gently.

Now prepare the peppers by slicing off the stalk ends and pulling out the core and the seeds. Run each one under cold water to make sure all the seeds are gone, then sit them upright in a small casserole (just so there's not too much room for them to keel over). When the rice is cooked, add it to the meat, etcetera, in the frying pan and stir well to combine everything. Taste to check the seasoning at this point.

Now spoon the mixture into the each of the peppers—pack it down well to get as much in as you can—put the rest of it all around the base of the peppers. Finally put a teaspoon of tomato purée on top of each stuffed pepper and pour the rest of the tin of tomatoes all over. Cover the casserole, and cook in the oven for 40–45 minutes or until the peppers are tender when tested with a skewer.

Salted Lamb with Marinade (Serves 4)

1½ lb middle neck of lamb (700 g)
1 oz sea salt (25 g)
2 tablespoons treacle
½ pint light ale (275 ml)
½ teaspoon dried sage

Dip the lamb lightly in the salt and shake off any excess. Place in a roasting tin and bake at gas mark 6 (400 °F, 200 °C) for 40 minutes until crispy. Drain on kitchen paper. They are just as good served cold as hot so you could chill them at this stage. Heat the remaining ingredients until well blended. To serve, cold dip the meat in the marinade for a couple of minutes and then arrange in a serving dish with pasta and pepper salad and serve the chilled marinade separately.

For the salad: Cook 8 oz pasta bows (225 g) in boiling water until just tender. Drain and rinse in cold water. Toss in a well-seasoned French dressing while roasting the lamb, then stir in 1 green and 1 red pepper (both diced) and 1 teaspoon coriander seeds. Chill before adding the cold lamb.

Alex Barker

Kentish Chicken Pudding   (Serves 6)

When there's frost outside, a pudding in a basin fits cosily into the warm-them-up, feed-them-up scheme. There's a warm and satisfying country flavour about chicken—or it could be rabbit—and bacon under a crust cap.

For the suet crust:
8 oz self-raising flour (225 g)
1 level teaspoon salt
3 oz shredded suet (75 g)
¼ pint water (150 ml)

For the filling:
½ lb unsmoked back bacon, cut in a piece (225 g)
1 lb uncooked chicken (or turkey) meat (450 g)
1 large onion, skinned and chopped
salt and pepper
1 tablespoon chopped parsley
¼ pint water (150 ml)

Mix together the flour, salt and suet. Add enough water to mix to a soft dough. Turn on to a floured surface and knead lightly until smooth. Roll out ⅔ of the pastry into a circle large enough to line a 2½ pint (1.4 litre) greased pudding basin. Line basin with pastry. Rind the bacon and cut into fork sized pieces, treat chicken meat in the same way. Mix together with onion, salt, pepper and parsley. Place mixture in lined bowl. Add water. Roll out remaining pastry to make a lid. Damp edges and place lid in position. Press pastry edges well together. Cover with a layer of greased greaseproof paper and kitchen foil. Boil the pudding for about 2½ hours in a large saucepan with a tight fitting lid and enough water to come half way up the basin.

Margaret Coombes.

Chicken Casserole (Serves 3–4)

A complete meal, this dish needs only a green salad as accompaniment.

3 lb roasting chicken (1.5 kg)
1 onion
1 carrot
1 stalk celery
6 oz noodles (175 g)
¼ lb flat mushrooms (110 g)
1 oz butter (25 g)
¼ pint sour cream (150 ml)
1 dessertspoon flour
1 lb tomatoes (450 g)

Poach the chicken with the halved onion, carrot and celery. Drain well and cut in large pieces, discarding skin and bone and reserving stock. Cook the noodles and drain, put them in the bottom of a buttered casserole, adding sea salt and black pepper. Toss the sliced mushrooms in the butter and lay over the noodles. Place the chicken pieces on top.

Beat the cream until smooth, stir in the flour, and heat slowly in a pan, adding ¼ pint (150 ml) of the strained chicken stock. When smooth and blended, pour over the chicken, mushrooms and noodles, making a few holes in the noodles with the handle of a wooden spoon to allow the sauce to penetrate. Top with a layer of sliced tomatoes and bake for 20 minutes at gas mark 4 (350 °F, 180 °C). (Alternatively, make in advance and reheat for 45 mintues at gas mark 3 (325 °F, 170 °C.)

Arabella Boxer.

Summer Chicken with Mint and Lemon
(Serves 6)

A simple but succulent dish of golden chicken with an exciting Middle-Eastern flavour. If your garden is overgrown with mint this is one good way to use it.

6 breast joints of chicken (I usually ask the butcher to cut them in half making twelve small pieces)
juice of 1 lemon
2–3 tablespoons olive or sunflower oil
2 large cloves garlic, crushed
1 teaspoon powdered turmeric
2–3 teaspoons powdered cumin
a large handful of fresh mint leaves, chopped finely
1 carton plain yoghurt

In a small bowl mix together the lemon juice, olive oil, crushed garlic, turmeric, cumin, salt and black pepper. Rub or paint (with a pastry brush) this mixture all over the chicken pieces. Lay them in a wide, preferably shallow, ovenproof dish. Pour over any extra oil and lemon mixture. If possible, leave to marinate for an hour or more at room temperature. Sprinkle the chopped mint leaves all over and some underneath the chicken pieces. Cover the dish with foil or a lid and cook in the centre of the oven at gas mark 4 (350 °F, 180 °C) for 1–1¼ hours. Before serving spoon the yoghurt roughly on top of the chicken. Serve with new potatoes or long grain rice and a mixed salad.

Josceline Dimbleby

Rabbit with Three Herbs (Serves 4)

This is a very aromatic dish.

1 jointed fresh rabbit
1 onion
2 teaspoons dried thyme
½ teaspoon savory
½ teaspoon wild thyme (or use more ordinary thyme and parsley)
1 tablespoon butter
1 tablespoon olive oil
4 oz mushrooms (110 g)
1 glass white wine
light chicken or veal stock
salt, pepper
flour and butter for thickening the sauce
a dash of cream if a less peasanty dish is wanted

Roll the rabbit pieces in seasoned flour. Chop the onion. Heat the oil and butter, brown the floured rabbit pieces, remove these and soften the onions, return the meat and add the sliced mushrooms. Pour on the white wine and enough stock just to cover. Add the herbs, season with salt and pepper and simmer until tender, ¾–1 hour. Strain and thicken the sauce with a nut of butter worked into a paste with a level tablespoon of flour. Stir this paste into the juice until it is all dissolved. Finish by stirring in a little cream and cook on until the flour has thickened the sauce.

Caroline Conran.

Rabbit and Celery in Cider (Serves 4)

One small wild rabbit and a little bacon can make a fairly cheap and substantial meal for four people. Make it just a little bit special by adding a dash of cider.

1 wild rabbit
2 tablespoons seasoned flour (preferably wholemeal)
1 oz bacon fat or pork dripping (25 g)
4 oz lean bacon pieces, diced (110 g)
3 large sticks celery, diced
1 medium onion, thinly sliced
¼ pint still, dry cider (150 ml)
1 tablespoon chopped mixed parsley and sage

Joint the rabbit. Cut all the meat from the bones and dice it into small pieces. Toss the meat in the seasoned flour. Melt the fat in a sauté pan or large frying pan on a low heat. Put in the bacon, celery and onion and cook them until the onion is soft. Remove them and set them aside. Raise the heat and add a little more fat if necessary. Put in the pieces of rabbit and fry them until they are brown, moving them around all the time so they don't stick together. Pour in the cider and bring it to the boil. Stir in the herbs, season and replace the vegetables and bacon. Cover the pan and cook on the lowest heat possible for 1 hour.

Lapin Provençal

(Serves 4–5)

This recipe is equally good with chicken. Use a jointed chicken or 5 chicken joints.

6 oz belly pork or streaky bacon (175 g)
1 rabbit, jointed
2 tablespoons cooking oil
½ lb onions (225 g)
½ a red pepper and ½ a green (or one of either)
14 oz tin tomatoes (400 g)
2 level teaspoons Herbs de Provence (includes thyme, marjoram,
    parsley, basil, chervil and lavender) or ordinary dried mixed herbs
1 level teaspoon French mustard
salt and pepper

Remove any rind or gristle from the pork and cut into cubes. Wash and dry the rabbit joints. Heat the oil in a frying pan and add the pork cubes. Fry over a brisk heat until they are nicely browned then put them into an ovenproof casserole. Fry the rabbit joints for a few minutes on each side until they are golden brown and add to the casserole.

Peel and slice the onions. Remove the core from the peppers and slice them. Reduce the heat slightly and gently fry the onions and peppers until soft. Stir in the tomatoes and their juice and sprinkle the herbs and French mustard over the top, then season carefully and bring to the boil.

Pour this over the meat and put on the lid. Cook in a low oven at gas mark 2 (300 °F, 150 °C) for 1¼–1½ hours, until the rabbit is tender. Serve with plenty of fresh crusty French bread and perhaps a bottle of wine from Provence.

Mary Meredith

Jugged Hare

(Serves 6–8)

All over Britain I find a longing to know more about our traditional dishes. This is particularly so in the younger generation and a jugged hare is an ideal method of cooking this particular game. Modern liquidisers make it easy to make a smooth purée of the liver.

1 jointed hare with the blood if possible
1–2 tablespoons vinegar
1–2 onions
2 carrots
2 oz dripping or lard (50 g)
2 oz flour (50 g)
¼ pint port wine (150 ml)
1–2 tablespoons redcurrant jeily
seasoning

For the stuffing:
2 oz shredded suet or melted butter (50 g)
½ teaspoon mixed herbs
grated rind and juice of ½ a lemon
4 oz soft breadcrumbs (110 g)
1 egg
seasoning
2–3 tablespoons chopped parsley

Put the liver of the hare on to cook in salted water and boil steadily for about 30 minutes. This will give you good flavoured stock. Soak the hare in cold water to which the vinegar has been added. Fry the chopped onion and carrots in the dripping, stir in the flour, add enough stock and water to give 1½ pints (900 ml). Bring to the boil and cook until thickened. Stir in the blood of the hare, the port wine, redcurrant jelly and seasoning. Mash the liver, rub through a sieve or put into the liquidiser and add to the gravy. The gravy may be sieved if wished before using. Cover the joints of hare with this sauce and cook very slowly for about 3 hours in either a covered casserole in the centre of a slow oven, gas mark 1–2 (275–300 °F, 140–150 °C), or in a heavy saucepan. The stuffing balls should be cooked, as in the recipe below, earlier, then placed on top of the sauce to heat for a few minutes before serving the hare.

To make the stuffing balls, blend all the ingredients together and form into small balls. Bake for approximately 20 minutes towards the top of a moderately hot oven, gas mark 5–6 (375–400 °F, 190–200 °C).

Arrange the jugged hare in the hot dish, top with the stuffing balls and serve with redcurrant jelly.

Note: You can fry the uncooked hare in hot dripping or lard before cooking the vegetables, but I find it absorbs the sauce better if simply taken from the water and vinegar, dried well on kitchen paper, then added to the sauce.

Marguerite Patten

Pigeons Stewed with Lettuces

Pigeons are often tough little birds, but in the country there are often a great many to be disposed of. Older birds make a good country dish cooked in the following way with lettuces.

For each pigeon you need:
2 cos lettuces
a cupful of meat or chicken stock
1 rasher of bacon
parsley and other herbs
2 shallots
salt and pepper
1 egg yolk
lemon juice

Blanch the pigeons in boiling water for 5 minutes and cut them in half. Then blanch the lettuces. Cut the lettuces down the middle without separating the two halves; spread them with a mixture of chopped shallots, parsley, herbs, salt and pepper. Put half a pigeon in the middle, tie them up, and place them in a pan lined with the bacon rashers. Pour the stock over them and simmer gently for about 1½ hours. Put them in a serving dish, thicken the sauce with a yolk of egg, squeeze in a little lemon juice and pour over the pigeons.

Elizabeth David

Offal

Chicken Liver Sauce for Pasta

(Serves 4)

This is a superb sauce for any kind of pasta. The rich flavour belies its low cost—just half a pound of chicken livers is needed to serve 4 people. It freezes well.

8 oz chicken livers (225 g)
2 medium onions, finely chopped
4 tablespoons oil and 1 oz butter or margarine (25 g)
1 level tablespoon chopped parsley
1 teaspoon dried mixed Italian herbs
a pinch each of cayenne and black pepper
1 level teaspoon each of salt and sugar
4 tablespoons dry wine—red or white (optional)
1 green pepper, seeded and finely diced
1 medium can Italian tomatoes or tomato juice
1 chicken bouillon cube
1 level tablespoon cornflour mixed with 2 tablespoons water

Cook the onion in the mixed fats until soft and golden, keeping the lid on the pan. Take off the lid, add the sliced livers and blend with the onion. Sauté until livers are no longer pink. Add all the remaining ingredients except the cornflour and water. Cover and simmer for about 20 minutes (longer will do no harm). Mix the cornflour with the cold water, then add to the pan. Bubble for 3 minutes. Serve over noodles, spaghetti or long macaroni. Serves 4 for a main course, with 1 lb pasta (450 g).

Evelyn Rose

Liver Vénitien

This way of cooking liver was shown to me by an old Italian cook. Gino's insistence on the importance of removing the skin from the liver, cutting it meticulously and cooking for only a very short time is the secret of this delicious recipe.   M.D.

1¼ lb lambs' liver, sliced (600 g)
1 tablespoon flour
3 oz butter (80 g)
1 medium onion, sliced
2 tablespoons wine vinegar
1 glass white wine
1 tablespoon chopped parsley

Remove the skin and ducts from the liver, cut in julienne strips, ½ x 4 inches (1 x 10 cm) and roll in seasoned flour. Melt ⅓ of the butter in a heavy frying pan, add the onion and cook until golden; moisten with the vinegar. Allow the contents of the pan to bubble gently until the vinegar has evaporated, then drop in the remaining butter, increase the heat under the pan and sauté the liver briskly for 3-5 minutes. Season, add the wine and herbs and reboil. Serve at once with a saffron pilaff.

Rosemary Hume
Muriel Downes

Liver Valencia

(Serves 4)

Liver is nutritious and delicious if cooked well, but over-cooking makes it tough and tasteless. This recipe is good enough to serve to guests and really quick to cook.

1 lb lambs' liver (450 g)
3 level tablespoons plain flour
salt and pepper
1 bunch spring onions
4 rashers streaky bacon
2 oz margarine (50 g)
¼ pint chicken stock (150 ml)
1 rounded teaspoon tomato purée
2 tablespoons dry sherry (optional)

to garnish: chopped spring onion tops or parsley

to serve: boiled rice

Slice liver into thin strips. Season flour with salt and pepper and use to coat liver. Wash and trim roots and tops from onions, cut onions into chunky pieces. Cut bacon into pieces, discarding rind and bone. Melt margarine in a frying pan. Add spring onions and bacon and fry for 2 minutes. Add liver and fry quickly until browned. Stir in stock, tomato purée and sherry, if using. Bring to boil then reduce heat and cook gently, stirring occasionally for a further 5 minutes. Serve sprinkled with chopped spring onion tops or parsley with boiled rice.

Frances M. Walcott

Creamed Kidneys with Ginger

(Serves 4)

These are also good served hot, piled into rich shortcrust tart cases.

6 calves' or lambs' kidneys
2 oz butter (50 g)
¼ pint thick cream (150 ml)
¼ teaspoon ground ginger
4 oz button mushrooms (110 g)
2 tablespoons Madeira or medium sherry
salt and freshly milled pepper

Skin and trim the kidneys; slice them thinly. Wipe and slice the mushrooms. Melt the butter in a skillet or frying pan until foaming and 'quiet'. Quickly fry the kidneys, seasoning lightly and adding the ginger. Remove with a draining spoon to a warm serving dish. Toss the mushrooms in the remaining pan juices, adding a little more butter if necessary. Pour in the cream and Madeira: cook until unctuous.

Pour this sauce over the waiting kidneys and serve on brown bread croûtons or with wild rice or pasta.

Catalan Tripe (Callos à la Catalana)   (Serves 4–6)

In Britain offal is comparatively cheap, and is a rich source of protein. Tripe is often overlooked, as not everyone likes the usual 'tripe and onions'. This dish from Catalonia is a lot less bland and is delicious served with potatoes either boiled or baked in their skins.

2 lb tripe (1 kg)
1 bay leaf
a small piece of lemon
2–3 tablespoons olive or other vegetable oil
2 onions, finely chopped
4 small tomatoes, peeled and chopped (or a small can of tomatoes)
1 tablespoon flour
1 tablespoon tomato paste
2 cloves garlic
1 glass white wine
2 cups stock (from tripe)
1 teaspoon salt
pepper
4 tablespoons chopped parsley

Blanch tripe, wash and simmer with bay leaf and lemon in salted water until tender. Cut into neat pieces and reserve 2 cups of the stock. Heat the oil in a large heavy saucepan and sauté the onions and tomatoes for about 5 minutes, or until the onions are soft. Stir in 1 tablespoon flour and cook for 1–2 minutes more, stirring all the time. Add the stock, wine, tomato purée, crushed garlic and the pieces of tripe. Stir thoroughly, season and continue to simmer for 1 hour. Towards the end of the cooking time stir in plenty of chopped parsley.

Anna Macmiadhachain

Sweet and Sour Tripe (Serves 6)

2 lb pork tripe (900 g)
3 tablespoons vegetable oil
1 teaspoon salt
3 spring onion stalks, chopped
¼ pint good stock (150 ml)
3 slices root ginger
3 tablespoons soya sauce

For the garnish: 2 tablespoons coriander leaves (optional)

For the sauce:
1½ tablespoons sugar
3 tablespoons vinegar
3 tablespoons fresh orange juice
2 tablespoons tomato purée
1 tablespoon soya sauce
2 tablespoons sherry
1½ tablespoons cornflour, blended in 6 tablespoons water

Bring 4 pints (2.25 litres) water to boil in a large saucepan. Add tripe to parboil for 20 minutes and drain. Cut spring onions into 2 inch (5 cm) sections. Mix the ingredients for the sauce together until well blended.

Heat the tripe in 3 pints water (1.7 litres) until contents start to boil. Reduce heat and simmer gently for the next 1½ hours. Drain the tripe and cut into 2½ x ½ inch (6 x 1 cm) strips.

Heat oil in a flameproof casserole. Add the ginger, spring onions and salt. Stir them together for 1 minute. Add the tripe. Turn and mix it with the other ingredients in the pan. Sprinkle the contents with stock, and soya sauce. Turn and mix, and leave to simmer over low heat for the next ½ hour. Pour in the sauce mixture, turn the heat high. Turn and mix all the ingredients together until the sauce thickens. Leave to simmer for 5 minutes.

Bring the casserole to the table and sprinkle the contents with coriander leaves before serving. Another excellent dish to consume with rice.

Oxtail Stew with Guinness (Serves 4–6)

2½–3 lb oxtail cut into sections (1–1.25 kg)
2 oz dripping or lard (50 g)
seasoned brown flour
½ lb small turnips, scrubbed and halved (225 g)
½ lb baby carrots, scrubbed and left whole (225 g)
12 small onions, peeled and left whole
1 pint Guinness (570 ml)
½ pint fairly strong beef stock (275 ml)
1 tablespoon tomato paste
½ teaspoon thyme
1 bay leaf

For the garnish:
chopped parsley
1 clove garlic, very finely chopped

Heat the dripping in a large saucepan or casserole. Wipe the meat joints with kitchen paper then toss in the seasoned flour. Reserve the remaining seasoned flour. Fry a small batch at a time until well browned, then remove to a plate. Add the prepared vegetables to the pan and brown in the fat remaining in the pan before removing and reserving on a separate plate. Pour off the surplus fat from the pan then return the meat to the pan over the heat and sprinkle in a rounded tablespoon of the remaining seasoned flour. Stir and cook for 2 or 3 minutes to brown the flour before adding the Guinness and stock. Add the tomato paste and herbs and bring to simmering point. Adjust the heat so the contents of the pan cook at a very gentle simmer. Cover and cook for 1½ hours. Add the browned vegetables, re-cover and cook for a further 1–1½ hours or until the meat practically falls from the bone. Taste and season before serving with a thick dusting of chopped parsley into which there has been incorporated a very finely chopped clove of garlic.

Caroline Liddell

Beignets de Cervelle

At the time of writing sheeps' brains cost 15–20p a pair and seem to me a bargain buy from the butcher. Brains in black butter, à la Provençale, or marinated in vinaigrette, all make delectable eating, but this fritter recipe is the best I know for winning over those who feel squeamish about offal. I use the leftover egg yolks to make a remoulade sauce to accompany the fritters and usually serve steamed spinach with them too.

4 sets (i.e. 4 pairs) sheeps' brains
1 tablespoon vinegar
4 oz plain flour (110 g)
salt, pepper
2 tablespoons oil
2 egg whites
oil for deep frying

Soak the brains for 3 hours in cold salted water to help wash away chips of bone and blood. Then rinse under a cold running tap and gently pull away as much of the membrane and white opaque bits as you can without tearing the flesh. This takes time and must be done delicately. Put the brains into a saucepan, add a tablespoon of vinegar and cold water to cover. Bring gently to simmering point, cover and cook for 15 minutes. Drain, refresh, drain again and place under a weighted plate for 2 hours.

Make the batter by sifting and seasoning the flour, stirring in the oil and gradually incorporating 10 tablespoons tepid water. When smooth and the consistency of thick cream, set the batter aside in a cold place for 2 hours. When ready to cook, heat cooking oil to 350 °F (180 °C). Beat the batter and fold in the stiffly beaten egg whites. Slice the brains, dip into the batter and deep-fry for 2-3 minutes, until puffed up and golden. Drain well on kitchen paper and serve piping hot.

Philippa Davenport

Brain Salad

(Serves 4–6)

My favourite way of eating brains. They should be well chilled, and served with wholemeal bread.

1–1½ lb brains (500–750 g)
salt
vinegar
chopped chives or spring onions
chopped parsley
grated rind of a lemon
juice of a lemon
olive oil
pepper, sugar

Soak brains in plenty of water, to which you have added a tablespoon each of salt and vinegar. Leave for an hour at least, then carefully remove the fine membranes. Sometimes this is an easy job, sometimes not—but don't worry, absolute perfection is not required.

Rinse the brains. Slide them into a pan of simmering salted water, with a scant tablespoon of vinegar. Bring back to simmering point, and poach until firm—10–15 minutes. Do not allow the water to boil vigorously, as the brains might disintegrate.

When they are firm, remove them from the pan with a slotted spoon or skimmer and leave them to cool. Then refrigerate for at least an hour, or longer if you like, so that they can be neatly sliced or cut into half inch (1 cm) dice. Put them in a single layer on a serving dish. Scatter generously with chives, or spring onions, parsley and lemon rind. Mix the lemon juice with twice its quantity of olive oil: season with salt, pepper and a very little sugar. Taste and add a little more oil if you like, though the dressing should be piquant. Pour carefully over the brains so as not to dislodge the herbs into unevenness.

Serve as a first course (serves 6), or as part of a mixed hors d'oeuvre (8–10), or as a supper dish after soup (4–5).

Jane Grigson

Faggots

(Serves 6)

These balls of minced offal and lights wrapped in caul fat are often sold as 'savoury ducks'. They are easy and cheap to make at home and you can produce some startling flavours by varying the herbs and seasonings which are essential for good faggots.

1 lb pigs' liver (450 g)
1 lb pigs' fry (450 g)
2 onions
lard
4 oz breadcrumbs (100 g)
2 eggs
1 teaspoon dried sage
1 teaspoon strong mixed herbs
salt and pepper
a piece of caul fat

First soak the caul fat in a bowl of tepid water for a couple of hours until it softens. Meanwhile mince the liver, pigs' fry and onions and brown quickly in a frying pan with a little lard. Mix with the breadcrumbs, eggs, herbs and seasoning. Divide the mixture into balls, each weighing about 2 oz (50 g).

Cut the piece of caul fat into a number of small squares and wrap one square around each faggot. Pack the faggots close together in a roasting tin and bake for 30 minutes in the oven at gas mark 4 (350 ° F, 180 °C).

You can eat faggots hot or cold. The best accompaniment for a hot dish is dried or marrowfat peas, cooked until they are soft and mushy; to my mind these are much more suitable than fine-flavoured garden peas or petits pois. A jug of rich gravy poured over the faggots is all you need to complete the meal.

David Mabey

123

Brawn

(Serves 4–6)

Few butchers nowadays take delivery of whole carcasses so you may well have to order a pig's head. If this is so, buy the whole one, ask the butcher to chop it in half for you and make double the quantity. While you're involved in this fiddly job, make enough for a couple of days because the extra will keep well in the fridge or you can freeze it.

½ a fresh pig's head
salt and pepper
1 bay leaf
1 sprig of thyme
6 peppercorns
1 large onion
1 large carrot
2 celery stalks
ground mace
a few thin slices of cucumber

Wash the pig's head well, making sure the ear and nostril are clean, then soak it in salted water for 1 hour. Cut off the ear and remove the brains and tie them in a piece of muslin. Pour boiling water over the ear, leave to soak for 5 minutes, then scrape off the hair. Put the pig's head in a large pan with the ear, bay leaf, thyme and peppercorns. Skin the onion, scrape the carrots and scrub the celery and add them to the pan with 2 teaspoons of salt. Cover the head with cold water, bring it to the boil, then cover the pan and simmer for 3 hours or until the meat is very tender. Strain off the liquid and allow it to cool completely in the fridge. As soon as the head is cool enough to handle, cut the meat from the bones. Remove the skin from the tongue and slice the meat. Thinly slice the ear. Mix the meats together in a bowl. Remove the solidified layer of fat from the top of the stock and return the stock to a large pan. Add the brains, tied in muslin, bring to the boil and boil hard until it is reduced by half. Chop the brains and mix them with the other meats, seasoning the mixture with salt, pepper and mace. Arrange a few cucumber slices at the bottom of a round cake tin and pack the meat on top. Pour in some of the liquid to just cover the meat and stand a small plate inside the tin (or the loose base from a same-size cake tin). Weight the plate and leave the brawn to become cold and set. When ready to serve, quickly dip the mould into boiling water and invert on to a serving plate.

Kathie Webber

Vegetarian Dishes

Curried Rice and Lentils (Serves 4)

A comforting dish, this can be served with hardboiled eggs, vegetable stews, or for non-vegetarians, with grilled sausages and bacon.

6 oz brown lentils (175 g)
3 oz rice (75 g)
salt
1 large onion
1 tablespoon oil
1 oz butter
½ teaspoon ground coriander
½ teaspoon ground cumin
¼ teaspoon ground ginger
¼ teaspoon ground turmeric
¼ teaspoon ground chilli
black pepper

Pick over the lentils, wash well, and put in a pan with cold water to cover. Bring to the boil and simmer for about 35 minutes, until almost soft. Add salt at this stage, and shake in the rice. Continue to cook until both lentils and rice are soft. Drain them, reserving the liquid. Slice the onion and brown slowly in the oil and butter. When starting to soften, add the spices and continue to cook, stirring often, for another 4–5 minutes. Add a drop of the lentil stock, just enough to moisten, and cook a few minutes longer. Stir in the drained rice and lentils, mix well, and cook gently for 5 minutes, adding a little more of the lentil stock until all is soft and slightly mushy. This can be eaten immediately or re-heated. It will thicken on cooling, so keep the lentil stock at hand to thin it. The flavour improves on standing for an hour or two.

Arabella Boxer.

Lentils and Anchovies

(Serves 4)

A delicious way of preparing brown lentils, from Catalonia.

1 lb brown lentils (450 g)
2 large onions
2 cans anchovy fillets
4 tablespoons olive oil
2–3 large cloves garlic
8 oz butter (use half mild flavoured margarine if liked) (225 g)
freshly ground black pepper

Carefully pick over the lentils to remove any stones or grit. This is most easily done by spreading them out a little at a time on a flat white plate or piece of paper.

Wash the lentils and cover them with cold water. Bring them to the boil, remove the pan from the heat and allow to stand for an hour. Roughly chop the peeled onions and put them into the lentils, bring them back to boiling point and simmer for 20–30 minutes, or until the lentils are tender without being mushy. In another saucepan heat the olive oil and put in the peeled and chopped garlic. Let it cook for a few minutes without browning. Strain the lentils. Gradually add the lentils to the hot oil, a ladle at a time, stirring continually, and when they are all in, lower the heat and add the butter cut in pieces and stir until it melts. Pound the anchovies to a paste in a mortar—this is easier if you take them from the tin stuck together in one piece and snip them up with scissors first. Use all the oil from the anchovies. Add this to the lentils and mix very thoroughly.

Serve with lots of freshly ground black pepper and green salad. This is also surprisingly good eaten cold.

Anna Macmiadhachain

Lentil and Vegetable Curry (Serves 3–4)

Pulses are delicious when cooked with spices, as in this recipe, which is typical of the type of main dish which, as a vegetarian, I make frequently. The lentils give excellent protein on their own, but they are even better value when combined with other types of protein such as cereal or dairy protein, the amino acids interacting to make more protein available to the body. This combination happens naturally if you serve the curry with rice (preferably brown), but if you don't like that, then a yoghurt and cucumber side salad or a chilled yoghurt pudding would do equally well.

The lentils, incidentally, are the usual red/orange supermarket type and don't need soaking beforehand.

4 tablespoons vegetable oil
2 medium onions, peeled and chopped
1 large carrot, peeled and diced
2 cloves garlic, crushed
½ teaspoon ground ginger
1 teaspoon turmeric
2 teaspoons ground cumin
2 teaspoons ground coriander
6 oz red lentils (175 g)
1 lb potatoes, peeled and cut into 1 inch (2.5 cm) dice (450 g)
8 oz can tomatoes (225 g)
1 pint vegetable stock (570 ml)
1 teaspoon sea salt
freshly ground black pepper
juice of ½ a lemon

Heat 3 tablespoons of the oil in a large saucepan and fry half the onion and all the carrot for 10 minutes until golden. Add the garlic, ginger, turmeric, half the cumin and half the coriander; stir for 2-3 minutes, then add the lentils and cook for a further 2–3 minutes. Add the potatoes, tomatoes, vegetable stock, salt and a good grinding of pepper; bring up to the boil, then put a lid on the saucepan, turn down the heat and cook gently for about 30 minutes until the lentils are cooked, the vegetables tender and the liquid absorbed.

Heat the remaining tablespoon of oil in a small saucepan and fry the rest of the onion, coriander and cumin for 10 minutes. Add this mixture to the curry, together with the lemon juice, and correct seasoning with more salt and pepper if necessary before serving with brown rice and mango chutney.

Rose Elliot

Barbecued Soya Beans (Serves 4)

Natural soya beans taste far better than TVP and alone can make a main dinner dish. Here they are given a sauce similar in flavour to Chinese marinade for pork.

8 oz soya beans (225 g)
2 pints water (1.15 litres)
¾ pint stock (vegetable stock if you are vegetarian) (425 ml)
2 tablespoons tomato purée
2 tablespoons tamari sauce (the only real soya sauce—available from most wholefood stores)
2 teaspoons clear honey
1 tablespoon white wine vinegar
2 teaspoons chopped rosemary
1 clove garlic, crushed without salt
freshly ground black pepper

Put the soya beans into a saucepan with the water, cover them and soak them for at least 12 hours. Bring them slowly to the boil and simmer them on top of the stove (or in the oven if you already have it on for something else) for 3 hours. Drain the beans if necessary (you may find all the water has evaporated). Heat the oven to gas mark 4 (350 °F, 180 °C). Put the beans into a casserole. Mix all the other ingredients together and stir them into the beans. Cover, and put the casserole into the oven for 2 hours. Serve them with brown rice, fried Chinese-style with egg and a dash of tamari sauce.

Vegetable Cous-cous

(Serves 4)

Cous-cous from Arab Africa is less complicated to do than it sounds. The cous-cous is cooked in the steam of the simmering vegetables, then the vegetables are served on top of the cous-cous. Cous-cous is a kind of coarse semolina.

4 oz cous-cous (110 g)
¾ pint vegetable stock (425 ml)
4 oz chick peas (110 g)
4 button onions, peeled
2 leeks
1 carrot, peeled
1 stick celery
2 courgettes
4 tomatoes, peeled
a pinch of saffron or a few shreds soaked in a tablespoon of water
1 dessertspoon chopped parsley
1 teaspoon chopped mint
salt and freshly ground black pepper
a pinch of dried oregano

For the sauce:
1 teaspoon cumin
1 teaspoon ground coriander
½ teaspoon chilli powder
2 tablespoons tomato purée
2 tablespoons hot stock

Soak the chick peas in cold water overnight. Drain them and simmer in fresh salted water until tender—about 2 hours. Drain well.

Cover the cous-cous with 8 fl oz cold water (225 ml) and leave to absorb the liquid for 10 minutes.

Thickly slice the leeks, carrot, celery and courgettes. Put the stock, salt, pepper and onions in large pan. Bring slowly up to the boil and add the leeks, carrots and celery.

Set the cous-cous to steam *above* the cooking vegetables.

134

(Ideally it should be put in a muslin-lined steamer or special cous-cousine, but a J-cloth fitted in a wire sieve will do.) Put the sieve in place, cover, using foil or a cloth to prevent the steam escaping too much, and simmer for 30 minutes.

Add the courgettes to the vegetable liquid. Fork the cous-cous to remove any lumps and return the lid. Cook for 10 minutes.

Add the tomatoes, mint, parsley and oregano to the vegetable mixture and again cover and cook for 10 minutes. Pour the cous-cous into a dish and keep warm.

Add the chick peas and saffron (with its water if soaked) to the vegetables and heat for 2 minutes. Drain off some of the stock. Mix two tablespoons of hot stock with the cumin, coriander, chilli powder and tomato purée.

Spread the cous-cous over a flat serving dish and pile the vegetables, with a cupful or so of stock, on the top. Serve the spiced stock separately.

Prudence Leith

Spinach Cutlets (Serves 4)

Serve these cutlets as a main course with boiled new potatoes or chips and a green salad. They are also very good accompanied by a light, fresh tomato sauce.

2 lb fresh spinach or spinach beet (perpetual spinach) (900 g)
1 medium onion, finely chopped
butter
1 large egg
fine dry breadcrumbs
salt and freshly ground black pepper
freshly grated nutmeg
oil or bacon fat, for frying

Wash the spinach carefully and strip off stalks and any thick ribs. Pack the leaves into a heavy pan, cover tightly and cook for 7–10 minutes, or until the leaves are tender. Cool spinach until it can be handled, then squeeze out as much moisture as possible between the palms of your hands. Chop spinach finely or put it through a mincer.

Simmer the onion in 1 oz butter (25 g) until soft and lightly coloured. Add to the spinach, together with the egg and 2 oz dry breadcrumbs (50 g). Knead ingredients together until smoothly blended. Season to taste with salt, pepper and nutmeg.

Shape mixture into 8 oval cutlets and coat them with dry breadcrumbs. Fry the cutlets in a mixture of butter and oil, or bacon fat, until the crumbs are crisp and golden, and the cutlets are heated through. Serve immediately.

Helena Radecka

Polish Baked Mushrooms

(Serves 4 as a first course or 2 as a main course)

This is particularly good for vegetarians and is nutritious and filling. Serve a good crisp mixed green salad with lemon dressing as a side dish.

½ lb flat mushrooms (225 g)
2 teaspoons lemon juice
1 tablespoon onion, minced fine
3 tablespoons unsalted butter
¼ teaspoon salt
a pinch of freshly ground pepper
1 tablespoon plain flour
2 tablespoons grated Parmesan
8 fl oz double cream (225 ml)
2 egg yolks, lightly beaten
2 tablespoons fine white breadcrumbs

Pre-heat the oven to gas mark 7 (425 °F, 250 °C).

Butter 4 individual ramekins or 1 small soufflé dish. Wipe the mushrooms and cut off their stems. Slice thinly and sprinkle with the lemon juice to prevent discolouration. In a saucepan with a tightly fitting lid simmer the mushrooms and onion in 1 tablespoon butter until soft. Season with salt and pepper. Stir in the flour and grated Parmesan cheese and cook for about 3 minutes. Turn into prepared dishes. Mix the cream and egg yolks together and pour over the mushrooms. Sprinkle with the breadcrumbs and dot with the remaining butter. Place the ramekins in a shallow baking dish half filled with water and bake in the pre-heated oven for about 10 minutes, or until golden brown. Serve immediately.

Potatoes with Red Mojo
Sauce (Salsa de Mójo Rojo)   (Serves 4)

It is about time the British got over their traditional aversion to garlic. Not only is it a source of warm and subtle flavour (used with discretion that is), but it also possesses considerable medicinal and blood-cleansing properties.

The following sauce is for real garlic fanciers, however, and will probably guarantee an end to all social life for at least a day after eating, except of course with those who partook at the same time.

It comes from the Canary Islands and is served with tiny potatoes boiled in very little salty water until well wrinkled. These are called 'papas arrugadas'—wrinkled potatoes. It is also used to accompany a dish of boiled salt cod, potatoes and sweet potatoes, which is known as 'Sancocho' and is a top favourite in all the Islands.

1½ lb small potatoes (750 g)
2 or 3 large cloves garlic
1 teaspoon cumin seed
1 teaspoon paprika
olive oil (or other vegetable oil)
vinegar
a pinch of thyme

Peel the garlic and crush it in a mortar with the cumin seeds. This takes time as the garlic should be really well pulped. When this is done add the paprika and thyme and pound a little more. Then slowly add olive oil, stirring well. Add about 2 teaspoons of vinegar, and when you have about a cup of sauce transfer it from the mortar to another bowl. Slowly stir in about ⅓ cup warm water, or more if you find the sauce too strong. Cool thoroughly before serving.

To prepare the potatoes, choose evenly sized small potatoes, scrub them and boil with a lot of salt in a very little water. When the water has almost evaporated and the potatoes are tender they are ready. To serve put into an earthenware bowl and dip into the sauce. Each person peels their own. This can be served as an hors d'oeuvre; in the Canaries it is a popular 'tapa'.

Anna Macmiaidhachain

Spiced Cauliflower with Rice

(Serves 6)

Subtle use of spices can transform familiar vegetables—here cauliflower owes its golden yellow colour to turmeric, its special flavour to those light mellow spices, coriander and cumin. Together they lift it into the sort of dish that's superb just on its own.

1 level teaspoon each of cumin seed, coriander seed, mustard seed
    and salt
½ level teaspoon turmeric
a pinch of cayenne pepper
2 tablespoons oil
1¼ lb cauliflower (550 g)
½ lb carrots (225 g)
½ lb onion (225 g)
2 oz cooking apple (50 g)
4 fl oz water (100 ml)
2 x 5⅓ oz cartons natural yoghurt (2 x 151 g)
8 oz long grain rice, freshly cooked (225 g)

Grind the spices with the salt in a pestle and mortar (or crush by using the end of a plain wooden rolling pin in a strong bowl). Heat the oil in a pan and add all the spices. Cook gently for 2 minutes. Discard some of the thick stem from cauliflower, and divide the head into small florets. Pare carrots and thinly slice. Skin onion and chop. Peel and dice the apple. Add the prepared vegetables and apple to the pan. Cook gently, stirring, for 5 minutes. Add the water and yoghurt. Stir well, cover lightly and simmer for about 10 minutes or until the vegetables are tender but still with a little bite. Serve on a bed of freshly cooked rice.

Margaret Coombes.

Nutty Cabbage

(Serves 4)

One of my favourite feasts consists of individual cheese soufflés followed by this delicately flavoured cabbage dish plus a few slices of hot garlic sausage, then Rich Rice Pudding. Stuffing the cabbage sounds a bit complicated on paper but in practice it's quite easy providing the cabbage has large, firm, crinkly leaves. You can ring the changes by adding to the stuffing or replacing some of the nuts with leftover cooked rice or minced meat, or you could accompany the cabbage with a garlicky tomato sauce.

1 x 2–2½ lb Savoy cabbage (approximately 1 kg)
1 very small onion
3 oz butter (75 g)
4 tablespoons chopped parsley
3 tablespoons fresh breadcrumbs
3 oz chopped nuts (75 g)
the zest of a small lemon
2 eggs
salt and freshly ground black pepper

Trim the cabbage stalk, reserve 6–8 outside leaves and shred the remainder. Gently cook the shredded cabbage and finely

140

chopped onion in butter, stirring frequently, for 20 minutes or until golden. Away from the heat, add the parsley, bread-crumbs, nuts, lemon zest and lightly beaten eggs. Mix well and season generously. Line a mixing bowl with butter muslin. Arrange the reserved cabbage leaves stalk end downwards in the bowl. Overlap the leaves slightly so there are no gaps. Pile the cabbage mixture into the centre of the leaves. Pull up the cloth round the cabbage and tie securely with string, so that the original tight cabbage shape is re-formed. Lower it into a pan of salted boiling water and cook for about 20 minutes. Then carefully unwrap and turn the cabbage on to a serving dish.

Philippa Davenport

Polish Cabbage with Noodles
(Serves 4–6)

1 large green (English) cabbage
½ lb noodles (225 g)
2–3 onions
salt, pepper
butter

Bring two pans of water to the boil, well salted.

Quarter the cabbage, cut away the thicker part of the core, wash the quarters well and drop them into one pan. Into the other put the noodles, stirring them around to prevent them from sticking together. Melt an ounce of butter in a frying pan and soften the onions, peeled and cut downwards into slivers, until tender and transparent.

When the cabbage is just tender, drain it very well, cut it up a little with a knife and add an ounce or more of butter. Add the onions together with their butter and let everything sit over a low heat for 10 minutes or so stirring from time to time so that any extra liquid evaporates. This makes the final result more mellow.

Meanwhile, drain the cooked noodles very well, stir them into the cabbage and season extravagently with freshly ground black pepper, and with salt if it is needed.

Caroline Conran.

Red Cabbage and Mushroom Pudding (Serves 4)

For the pastry:
8 oz self-raising flour (225 g)
½ level teaspoon salt
4 oz shredded suet (110 g)
water to mix

For the filling:
½ a red cabbage, shredded
6 oz mushrooms, sliced (175 g)
2 oz butter (50 g)
2 oz flour (50 g)
½ pint milk (275 ml)
salt and pepper
a pinch of bay powder

Make the pastry by mixing the flour, salt and suet and combining with enough water to give a pliable dough. Roll out ⅔ of the mixture and line a greased 1 pint (570 ml) pudding basin. Blanch the cabbage in boiling water for 3 minutes and drain well. Sauté the mushrooms lightly in the melted butter and then remove and mix with the cabbage. Add the flour to the butter and mix to a paste before adding the milk gradually, stirring all the time to make a smooth sauce. Flavour with salt and pepper and bay powder. Mix with the cabbage and mushrooms. Spoon into the pastry lined bowl and top with the remaining pastry, rolled to fit as a lid. Seal the edge of the pastry with water. Bake for 30-40 minutes, at gas mark 6 (400 °F, 200 °C).

Alex Baker

Nut and Cream Cheese Bake

(Serves 6–8)

Here's a delicious mingling of rich flavours without introducing any meat . Serve it with a fresh tomato and watercress salad for a simple yet substantial main meal dish.

4 oz butter or margarine (100 g)
1 lb onions, skinned and chopped (450 g)
1 lb courgettes, wiped and sliced (450 g)
6 oz mushrooms, wiped and sliced (175 g)
6 oz wholemeal breadcrumbs (175 g)
12 oz cream cheese (350 g)
2 oz nibbed almonds (50 g)
2 oz walnut pieces, chopped (50 g)
2 oz dessicated coconut (50 g)
2 level tablespoons tomato paste
a few drops of Tabasco sauce
½ level teaspoon each of dried rosemary, sage and marjoram
salt and freshly milled pepper

Melt the butter in a large frying pan. Sauté the onions and courgettes together until the onion is transparent. Add the mushrooms and continue to sauté for 1–2 minutes. In a large basin, combine the vegetable mixture with all the remaining ingredients until evenly blended. Turn into a 2¾ pint ovenproof dish (1.6 litre). Cover and bake at gas mark 5 (375 °F, 190 °C) for 40 minutes. Ten minutes before the end of the cooking time remove the lid to brown the surface.

Margaret Coombes.

Vegetables and Salads

Cabbage with Caraway

Any cabbage will do. The best is the Savoy because it is both crisp and green.

shredded cabbage
salt and freshly ground black pepper
butter
caraway seeds
lemon juice
soured cream

Boil the cabbage in plenty of fast boiling water for 2–3 minutes or until just tender. Drain well. Toss immediately in melted butter, adding salt, pepper, lemon juice, and caraway seeds to taste. Put into a serving dish and fork in the soured cream.

Prudence Leith

Sour-Sweet Cabbage (Serves 4–6)
(Cavoli in Agrodolce)

1 large green cabbage
olive oil and/or bacon fat
1 small onion
2–3 large ripe peeled tomatoes (or a small spoonful of concentrated purée diluted with a little water)
salt and pepper
1 large tablespoon wine vinegar
1 tablespoon soft white sugar

Wash the cabbage and cut it into thin strips, discarding the hard parts of the stalks in the centre of the leaves.

In a roomy saucepan, heat a little olive oil or bacon fat, or a mixture of the two. In this sauté the chopped onion. When it is golden add the tomatoes or purée, and when these are soft, add the cabbage. Stir it round; add salt and pepper and a large tablespoon of wine vinegar. Let it simmer for 20 minutes, stirring frequently with a wooden spoon. Five minutes before serving stir in a tablespoon of soft white sugar.

Elizabeth David

Sweet Glazed Carrots (Serves 4)

Some vegetables have a natural sweetness, carrots, onions and peas are good examples. If, in cooking, this sweetness is emphasised, the flavour of the vegetable is much more interesting. Carrots served in a glaze of butter, with a little sugar and onion added, taste very good indeed.

1 lb carrots (450 g)
½ an onion
1 bay leaf
2 teaspoons caster sugar
½ oz butter (10 g)
¼ pint water (150 ml)
salt and freshly milled pepper

Scrape the carrots and slice or cut in dice. Place in a saucepan and add the finely chopped onion, the bay leaf, sugar, butter, water and a seasoning of salt and pepper, cover with a lid, bring to a simmer and cook over a moderate heat. After about 15–20 minutes the carrots should feel tender. Remove the pan lid and allow any liquid remaining to boil and evaporate. When the carrots begin to fry in the butter glaze that remains, take them

148

off the heat. Toss the carrots in the shiny butter glaze and serve. A sprinkling of freshly chopped parsley looks pretty as a garnish.

Katie Stewart.

Mustard Glazed Turnips (Serves 6)

2 oz butter (50 g)
2 lb baby turnips, golfball size, peeled (900 g)
¼ pint chicken stock (150 ml)
1 teaspoon demerara sugar
salt and freshly ground black pepper
2 teaspoons Dijon mustard
2 tablespoons finely chopped parsley

In a large, heavy pan, melt the butter until frothy. Add the turnips, turning them over to coat them on all sides. Cook over moderate heat for about 10 minutes, shaking the pan frequently so that they turn an even, deep golden colour all over, rather like roast potatoes.

Turn the heat down to low. Pour in the stock and sprinkle the turnips with sugar, salt and pepper, to taste. Bring to simmering point; cover tightly and cook over a low heat, shaking the pan occasionally, for 20 minutes, or until the turnips feel tender when pierced with a sharp fork or skewer.

Lift the turnips out of the pan with a slotted spoon. Stir the mustard into the juices left in the pan and taste for seasoning, adding more salt, pepper or sugar if necessary. Then return the turnips to the pan and reheat them, swirling them around to coat them with the buttery glaze. Serve garnished with parsley.

Helena Radecho

149

Lemon Potatoes

(Serves 4-6)

Such a useful recipe, as it is a vegetable dish that can be completely prepared the day before it is required and just heated through and browned when the meal is to be served.

2 lb potatoes, peeled (900 g)
1½ oz butter (40 g)
1 medium onion, peeled and finely chopped
grated rind and juice of 1 lemon
2 level tablespoons chopped parsley
salt and pepper

Cut the potatoes into 1 inch cubes (2.5 cm), put them into a large pan, cover with cold water and bring to the boil. Simmer for 3 minutes then drain the pieces well. Melt the butter in the empty pan, add the chopped onion and fry it slowly until cooked but not coloured. Stir in the lemon rind and juice, chopped parsley, salt and pepper. Return the potatoes to the pan and toss them gently so they are evenly coated by the mixture. Turn the potatoes into a shallow ovenproof dish. They can be left at this stage in a cool place overnight.

Bake Lemon Potatoes in a moderately hot oven, gas mark 5 (375 °F, 190 °C) for 50 minutes to 1 hour or until they are golden brown and crispy on top. These potatoes are delicious served with roast pork.

Janet Warren

Paprika Potatoes

(Serves 4–6)

8 medium-sized raw potatoes
1 large onion
4 teaspoons paprika
2 oz butter or cooking fat (50 g)
water
salt

Chop the onion finely and fry it gently in the melted butter until it begins to turn golden. Stir in paprika and blend smoothly. Cut the peeled potatoes into cubes.

Add them to the onion mixture with a good pinch of salt and just enough water to cover them. Put a lid on the pan and cook slowly for 25–30 minutes.

For the original Austrian dish you should add a teaspoonful of caraway seeds before you pour in the water—but leave them out if you do not appreciate their flavour; you will still have a delicious dish.

Margaret Costa

Haricot Beans

(Serves 4)

(to serve with Roast Lamb)

Try this dish when you are next roasting a leg or shoulder of lamb. It makes an extraordinarily good alternative to the usual dish of potatoes or rice. If you find the flavour rather too strong for your taste, increase the beans by 2 or 3 oz (50–75 g) but do not disturb the balance of the sauce.

8 oz dried haricot beans (225 g)
1 oz lamb fat, finely chopped (25 g)
1 oz butter (25 g)
1 medium-sized Spanish onion, finely chopped
2 cloves garlic, crushed
14 oz tin Italian peeled tomatoes (400 g)
4–6 tablespoons juices from roasting tin
salt and freshly ground black pepper
finely chopped parsley to garnish (optional)

Soak the beans overnight, covered with cold water. Alternatively, if time is short, put the beans in a pan, cover with cold water and slowly bring to the boil. Simmer for 2 minutes, then cover the pan and leave the beans to soak for at least 1 hour.

Drain the soaked beans. Cover with plenty of fresh water; bring to the boil and simmer until soft but far from mushy, 30 minutes or a little longer, depending on age.

Meanwhile, in a heavy pan, fry the pieces of lamb fat (shaved from the joint before putting it into the oven) in butter until the fat runs. Remove the crisp pieces of lamb fat with a slotted spoon and in the resulting mixture of fats fry the onion and garlic until soft and golden. Pour in the can of tomatoes, together with their juices, and cook gently, uncovered, for 15 minutes, or until the tomatoes are reduced to a thick pulp. Cover the pan and put aside until needed.

When the beans are soft, drain them thoroughly. Mix them gently into the tomato sauce, together with a few tablespoons of the juices from the roast lamb, which should by now be nearing the end of its cooking time. Season generously with salt and pepper; cover and simmer gently for 30 minutes longer, stirring occasionally.

Sprinkle with chopped parsley if available and serve as an accompaniment to the roast lamb.

Helena Radecho

Sauerkraut (Serves 6–8)

A hearty dish for cold evenings, this is the perfect accompaniment to boiled bacon, pork chops, smoked or fresh sausages, or game.

2 x 28 oz tins sauerkraut (2 x 800 g)
1 Spanish onion
2½ oz beef dripping or butter (60 g)
2 rashers streaky bacon
10 juniper berries
sea salt and black pepper
1 teaspoon sugar
1 tablespoon flour
2½ fl oz soured cream (60 ml)

Empty the sauerkraut into a colander and rinse briefly under the cold tap, separating it with the fingers. Drain. Chop the onion and cook slowly in the fat until it starts to soften. Add the chopped bacon and continue to cook, stirring, until coloured. Add the drained sauerkraut and stir around until well mixed. Pour on hot water to almost cover, add the juniper berries, salt and pepper, and the sugar. Bring to the boil, cover the pan, and cook very slowly for 2 hours, either on top of the stove or in a low oven, gas mark 2 (300 °F, 150 °C). When the time is up, stir the flour into the soured cream and add to the casserole gradually, stirring constantly until smooth and slightly thickened. Add more salt and pepper as needed. This can with advantage be made a day in advance and reheated for 1 hour at gas mark 3 (325 °F, 170 °C).

Arabella Boxer.

Vegetarian Fried Rice

(Serves 5–6)

1 lb boiled rice (450 g)
4 eggs
1 teaspoon salt
2 medium onions
3 tablespoons oil
2 tablespoons mixed pickles
4 tablespoons green peas
4 tablespoons sweet corn
2 young carrots
½ a head of lettuce
4 tablespoons good stock
3 tablespoons butter
2 tablespoons soya sauce

Beat the eggs with salt for 10 seconds with a fork. Cut the onion into thin slices and the carrots into ¼ inch (½ cm) cubes. Chop the pickles into coarse grains. Tear the lettuce into small pieces.

Heat the oil in a medium saucepan. Add the onion and carrots. Stir them over a medium heat for 1 minute and leave to cook for 2 minutes. Add the peas, pickles and corn. Stir them together and leave to cook for 1 minute. Add the cooked rice, turning with the other ingredients in the pan. When well mixed, leave the contents to cook gently over a low heat for 3 minutes. Sprinkle with stock, turn the contents over, and continue to cook gently for 3–4 minutes.

Heat the butter in a small frying pan. When it has melted, pour in the beaten egg. Stir it around a few times, leave to cook over a low heat until set. Break up the egg, and add it to the rice and other ingredients in the saucepan, along with the shredded lettuce. Stir them together and sprinkle with soya sauce. Stir and turn once more, and the rice is ready to serve.

There should be enough rice to divide into 5–6 portions, to be served and consumed together with 2–3 other savoury dishes.

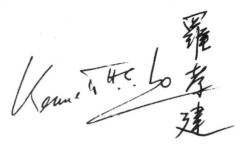

Mushroom Salad (Serves 4–6)

1 lb button mushrooms (450 g)
¼ pint dry white wine (150 ml)
1 teaspoon coriander seeds, crushed
1 tablespoon white wine vinegar
1 teaspoon coarse salt
½ teaspoon sugar
1 teaspoon French mustard
¼ pint olive oil (150 ml)
1 tablespoon chopped parsley
1 small onion, finely diced
6 black olives, pitted and chopped
freshly ground black pepper

Wipe the mushrooms and trim the stems level with the caps. Put the mushrooms and the wine in a saucepan with the crushed coriander seeds and cook, uncovered until the wine has practically all evaporated—shake the pan from time to time so the mushrooms cook evenly.

Whilst the mushrooms cook, prepare the dressing. Start with the vinegar and whisk in one ingredient after the other in the order they appear in the recipe. Taste and season as required.

Pour the dressing onto the hot mushrooms, leave to cool, then chill lightly in a refrigerator until ready to serve.

Serve as a starter with chicory or watercress or perhaps as an accompaniment to cold meats and jacket potatoes.

Caroline Liddell

Red Cabbage and Carrot Salad (Serves 4)

If you serve as many vegetables as possible raw, they will feed more people and will be far better for you. With the addition of a few spices or pickles even the most ordinary of vegetables can be made appealing.

½ a small red cabbage
2 medium sized carrots
1 large Bramley apple
2 large pickled Hungarian gherkins
3 tablespoons olive oil
1 tablespoon red wine vinegar
1 teaspoon dill seeds
1 clove garlic, crushed with a pinch of sea salt
freshly ground black pepper

Shred the cabbage. Grate the carrots on a coarse grater. Quarter, core and chop the apple. (Don't peel it—all the goodness lies

156

just under the skin.) Finely chop the gherkins. Put all these together in a salad bowl. Beat the oil, vinegar, dill, garlic and pepper together to make the dressing and fold them into the salad.

Oriental Rice Salad   (Serves 8)

¾ lb long-grain rice (350 g)
salt
lemon juice
4 oz green peas, cooked (100 g)
½ a green pepper, seeded, cored and finely diced
½ a red pepper, seeded, cored and finely diced
6 tablespoons finely chopped parsley
6 tablespoons finely chopped spring onions

For the dressing:
1 tablespoon lemon juice
½ a clove garlic, crushed
3 tablespoons olive oil
salt and freshly ground black pepper

Boil rice in plenty of salted water until tender but still very firm. (Add a little lemon juice to keep it white.) Drain thoroughly and allow to cool. In a serving bowl toss the rice with the peas, red and green peppers, parsley and spring onions.

To make the dressing, mix the lemon juice with the crushed garlic. Beat in the olive oil with a fork and season generously with salt and freshly ground black pepper. Pour the dressing over rice mixture; toss thoroughly and taste for seasoning, adding more salt, freshly ground black pepper, oil or lemon juice if necessary. Chill until ready to serve.

Auckland Pasta Salad (Serves 5–6)

Originally created for a series of cookery demonstrations I gave around the country, this recipe has now become a firm favourite with friends and family alike.

4 oz pasta shells (110 g)
4 oz carrots, peeled and grated (110 g)
4 oz Cheddar cheese, cubed (110 g)
1 small cauliflower, sprigged
1 oz salted peanuts (25 g)
1 dessert apple, cored and chopped
4 oz mushrooms, wiped and sliced (110 g)

For the dressing:
4 tablespoons cooking oil
1 tablespoon vinegar
a pinch of caster sugar
salt and pepper
a little French made mustard
2 level tablespoons chopped parsley

Put the pasta into a pan of boiling, salted water and cook it for 12–15 minutes or until a piece feels completely soft. Drain the shells and run cold water through them to remove any excess starch and separate the shells. Put the pasta into a bowl and stir through the carrot with the prepared cheese, cauliflower, apple and mushrooms, then add the peanuts.

Using a screw-topped jar, pour the oil and vinegar into it then add the sugar, seasoning, French mustard and parsley. Screw on the lid and shake well, so the ingredients emulsify. Pour the dressing over the salad and toss the ingredients well before the salad is served.

Janet Warren

Salade Russe

This salad is equally at home at a family supper and as part of a formal celebration buffet. Take great care not to overcook the vegetables so that they can be mixed and served without breaking down into a mush.

Cooked vegetables:
6 oz each of the following, cleaned, scraped or peeled as usual and
   cut into ¼ inch dice: carrot, parsnip, swede (175 g of each cut into
   ½ cm dice)
6 oz frozen green peas (175 g)
1½ lb potatoes (700 g)

Raw vegetables:
1 large carrot, coarsely shredded
½ medium sized parsnip (2–3 oz), coarsely shredded (50–75 g)
1 medium sized cooking apple, coarsely shredded
1 large pickled gherkin, finely diced (optional)
6 tablespoons diced celery
3 inch piece white of leek, sliced paper-thin (7.5 cm piece), or 3–4
   spring onions, finely chopped

For the dressing:
6 tablespoons oil—olive, corn or sunflower
1 tablespoon wine vinegar
juice of ½ a lemon
4 tablespoons thick home made mayonnaise
2 tablespoons finely chopped parsley
salt and freshly ground black pepper
sugar

For the garnish/decoration:
lettuce leaves
wedges of lemon, hard boiled egg, peeled tomato
black olives

Having prepared the diced carrot, parsnip and swede in separate dishes, get together a large mixing bowl, a colander and a slotted spoon. Bring a pan of lightly salted water to simmering point. Cook each batch of diced vegetables in the same water, one after the other, until just done, transferring them to the colander with the slotted spoon. The carrot will take about 8 minutes, the parsnip and swede about 5 minutes each. Give the peas barely the minimum time directed on the pack.

Peel the potatoes and cut them into slightly larger (about ⅓ inch, ¾ cm) dice. Rince any starch off with cold water. Bring another pan of salted water to the boil and cook the potatoes until just tender, testing a cube every minute. They will take between 4 and 5 minutes. Drain well in the colander, cool and add to the bowl of cooked vegetables.

Using a large fork, mix in the raw vegetables and continue to turn the salad over until all the ingredients are thoroughly mixed. Fold in the dressing ingredients, adding salt, pepper and about a teaspoon of sugar, to taste. The salad may now be served immediately or covered and left in the bottom of the refrigerator until the following day.

Serve in a lettuce-lined bowl, decorated according to your fancy.

Helena Radecho

Avocado and Cottage Cheese Salad

(Serves 2)

Although avocados are expensive, cottage cheese isn't, and so this protein-rich salad is not as extravagant as it sounds. The combination of varying shades of green, from the buttery yellow-green avocado to the vivid dark green watercress, makes this an attractive salad, and it's good served with thin slices of home made wholewheat bread and butter. When I can, I use my own home made cottage cheese for it: it's easy to do—see below—and far nicer than most of the shop varieties (and cheaper).

1 avocado pear
juice of ½ a lemon
8 crisp lettuce leaves
6 oz cottage cheese (175 g) (see below)
½ a bunch of watercress
1 small clove garlic, crushed
3 tablespoons olive oil
1 teaspoon wine vinegar
sea salt
freshly ground black pepper

Halve the avocado, remove peel and stone. Cut avocado into slices, put on a plate and sprinkle with the lemon juice to prevent discolouration. Arrange the lettuce leaves on two serving plates, place a pile of cottage cheese on top of the lettuce and arrange the watercress and avocado slices around the sides.

In a small bowl mix the garlic, oil, vinegar and any lemon juice remaining from the avocado; also salt and a good grinding of black pepper. Mix well. When ready to serve, pour the dressing over the cottage cheese and avocado platter so that it glistens appetisingly.

To make cottage cheese simply at home, put 2 pints milk (1.3 litres) into a large bowl and stir in 2 tablespoons yoghurt or soured cream. Cover with a clean cloth and leave in a warm place for 3-4 days until solid. Strain through a sieve lined with a double layer of clean butter muslin, then tie the muslin at the top and hang up for 12 hours to extract the remaining whey. Flavour with sea salt.

Rose Elliot

Solomongundi (Sallid Magundi)

This Tudor salad is surely England's answer to France's Salade Niçoise. It makes a more than substantial main course on a hot summer's day for either lunch outdoors or supper on the terrace. It is an ideal—and it you consider it carefully, cheap—way of entertaining a number of guests.

cold chicken or turkey
lettuce
cold cooked french beans
cold crisply-cooked carrot strips
anchovy fillets
green and black grapes
hardboiled eggs
button onions or spring onions
stoned raisins
flaked almonds
oil and vinegar dressing
plenty of freshly picked and chopped green herbs
lemon rind

As this salad is to be ad-libbed in the way that all salads should be, I suggest you start with the chicken or turkey meat as the main ingredient; shred this into striplets and arrange on a bed of lettuce, likewise shredded. Add the rest of the ingredients at will but somewhat abundantly!

Dress liberally with rich oil and vinegar dressing which has been spiked with finely grated lemon rind and sprinkle the finished platter with plenty of green herbs. Toss the whole mass together just before serving.

Michael Smith

Sabblesh Salad

(Serves 4–6)

Why is it that we don't serve more pasta salads in the summer? No potatoes to peel, an exciting texture and a very quick cooking time make these pasta based salads excellent and inexpensive hot weather dishes. As with all cold foods, garnishing is important; the finished dish should look cool and attractive and should be served chilled.

8 oz macaroni or pasta shells (225 g)
1 chicken stock cube
1 large tin tuna fish
7½ fl oz mayonnaise (225 ml)
2 tablespoons double cream
salt and freshly ground black pepper
1 green pepper
1 tablespoon finely chopped pimento
4 oz very firm, small button mushrooms (110 g)
½ pint water (275 ml)
juice of ½ a lemon
2 tender stalks of celery
6 black olives
1 tablespoon very finely chopped parsley or chives

Drain the oil off the tuna fish. Beat the oil, a few drops at a time, into the mayonnaise and beat in the cream. Season the mayonnaise with salt and freshly ground black pepper if necessary.

Cook the pasta until tender in boiling water to which a chicken stock cube has been added. As soon as the pasta is just tender (do not over-cook it), drain it in a sieve and run cold water through it. Drain well, add the mayonnaise while the pasta is still warm, and leave to cool.

Combine the lemon juice with the water, season with salt and pepper, bring to the boil and drop in the mushrooms (slice them unless they are very small indeed). Cook the mushrooms for three minutes, drain them well and leave to cool.

Remove the core and seeds of the green pepper and finely chop the flesh. Very thinly slice the celery stalks. Coarsely flake the tuna. Add the tuna, mushrooms, pimento, pepper and celery to the pasta and mix very lightly, taking care not to break up the ingredients. Turn into a serving dish and garnish with very fine slices of black olives. Sprinkle over the parsley or chives and serve well chilled.

Marika Hanbury Tenison,

Sillsalat

(Serves 4–6)

I have had the opportunity to try a variety of herring salads as my sister, who is married to a Norwegian and lives in Oslo, takes great pleasure in giving me different combinations of flavours with the fish. This is a favourite of mine. You can use either Bismark or Rollmop herrings.

¼ pint salad dressing or mayonnaise (150 ml)
1 medium cooked beetroot
1 dessert apple
4 medium boiled potatoes
6 oz cooked meat (beef, ham or pork) (175 g)
a little white wine vinegar
2 tablespoons orange juice
sugar to taste
2 pickled herrings
2 gherkins or a small pickled cucumber

To garnish:
lettuce, 1–2 hardboiled eggs and a little chopped dill

Put the salad dressing or mayonnaise into a basin. Peel and dice the beetroot and apple. Dice the potatoes and meat. Cover the beetroot with a little vinegar, leave for a short time then blend with the salad dressing or mayonnaise, together with the fruit juice and sugar. Flake the pickled herrings and chop the gherkins or cucumber. Mix all the ingredients together and spoon into a basin (to form a neat shape), leave for a short time then turn out, or shape without using the basin. Turn on to a bed of lettuce. Slice the hardboiled eggs and arrange round the mould. Top with the chopped dill.

Puddings

Oldbury Gooseberry Pies (Makes 4)

A Gloucestershire speciality, sometimes called Oldbury Tarts. They are made with hot-crust pastry, slightly sweetened, and filled with fruit rather than the more usual meat or game.

1 lb plain flour (450 g)
4 oz lard (100 g)
½ pint water (300 ml)
1 teaspoon caster sugar
½ lb gooseberries (225 g)
4 oz demerara sugar (100 g)

Put the flour into a bowl and mix with the caster sugar. Boil the lard and water in a saucepan until the lard is dissolved. Tip on to the flour and mix well until you have a workable dough. While it is still warm, but not uncomfortable to handle, roll it out and cut out a few circles using a saucer. Shape the discs into cases by raising the sides an inch or so, moulding and pressing the pastry with your hands. Fill the pastry cases with gooseberries which have been topped and tailed and sprinkle with demerara sugar.

Roll out some smaller pieces of dough to serve as lids for the pies, brush the sides of the pastry cases and fit the lids on top of the pies, pinching the edges together. Make a small hole in the centre of each lid and bake the pies for 25–30 minutes at gas mark 6 (400 °F, 200 °C). These pies can be served warm or cold with a jug of cream.

David Mabey

Pear and Chocolate Flan (Serves 4-6)

This recipe was voted the best flan of the year by the students and staff of the Cordon Bleu Cookery School in London for 1977.

For the chocolate pastry:
7 oz plain flour (200 g)
1½ oz cocoa (30 g)
4 oz butter (100 g)
4 oz caster sugar (100 g)
1 egg and 1 yolk
2–3 drops vanilla essence

For the filling:
3–4 ripe dessert pears
1 tablespoon vanilla sugar
2 tablespoons brandy

To finish:
egg white and caster sugar

First prepare the pastry. Sift the flour with the cocoa and a pinch of salt on to a board, make a well in the centre and in this place the other ingredients. Work to a firm paste with the fingertips and chill for ½ an hour before using. Peel, quarter and core the pears, sprinkle with the sugar and brandy. Cover and leave to macerate for ½ an hour. *Note*: If the pears are unripe, they *must* be poached in a vanilla flavoured syrup until tender and left to cool in the syrup before using.

Pre-heat the oven to gas mark 5 (375 °F, 190 °C). Roll out ⅔ of the pastry and line an 8–9 inch flan ring (20–23 cm). Drain the pears, arrange in the flan and reserve the juice. Roll out the remaining pastry with any trimmings and cut in ½ inch strips (1 cm); arrange these lattice fashion over the pears. Bake for about 35 minutes in the oven.

About 5 minutes before the tart is cooked, remove from the oven and brush lightly with egg white and dust with caster sugar. Return to the oven for a few minutes to frost the top. Serve with a bowl of whipped cream flavoured with the reserved pear juice.

Rosemary Hume

Southern Peanut Pie

(Serves 6)

When in Savannah in Georgia, I was taken to dinner at a beautiful 18th century mansion house called The Olde Pink House Restaurant which specialises in local dishes and Southern Creole cooking. The dessert trolley was magnificent with a number of American pies. This one was created by the dessert cook at the restaurant, Ann Arnold, a delightful lady who has been at The Pink House for 30 years.

For the pastry:
6 oz plain flour (175 g)
1½ oz margarine (40 g)
1½ oz lard (40 g)
cold water to mix

For the filling:
4 oz icing sugar (110 g)
4 level tablespoons crunchy peanut butter
1 oz granulated sugar (25 g)
3 rounded tablespoons cornflour
¾ pint milk (425 ml)
3 eggs
1 oz butter (25 g)
½ teaspoon vanilla essence
5 oz caster sugar (150 g)

Sift the flour into a bowl, add the fats cut into small pieces and rub in finely. Mix to form a firm dough with 9 teaspoons cold water. Turn out on to a floured board and knead lightly. Roll out and line an 8 inch ring (20 cm) set on a baking sheet or pie plate. Prick base of pastry and line with foil, fill with baking beans and bake in a moderately hot oven, gas mark 5 (375 °F, 190 °C) for 15 minutes. Remove foil and beans and return to oven for a further 5 minutes to dry out.

Meanwhile prepare the filling. Mix the icing sugar and peanut butter until well mixed and crumbly. Mix the granulated sugar and cornflour together, blend to a smooth paste with a little of the milk. Heat the remaining milk, pour on to the blended mixture, stir well, return to the saucepan and bring to the boil; cook, stirring, for 2 minutes. Cool slightly.

Separate the eggs, reserve the whites and beat the yolks into the milk mixture, with the butter and vanilla essence. Sprinkle ¾ of the peanut crumble mixture over the baked pie shell. Top with the custard mixture. Whisk the egg whites until stiff. Whisk in half the caster sugar, fold in the remainder. Pile meringue over custard mixture, sprinkle with remaining peanut mixture and cook in a moderate oven, gas mark 4 (350 °F, 180 °C) for 15 minutes.

Frances M. Walbrett

Tourte à la Citrouille (Serves 4)

This is an interesting dish, a bit of a curiosity. I find the combination of yellow pumpkin and black prunes beautiful as well as unexpectedly good.

1 lb peeled, de-seeded pumpkin (450 g)
2 oz sugar (50 g)
¼ pint fresh cream (150 ml)
20 prunes (soaked, cooked and stoned)
2 oz butter (50 g)

For the pastry:
4 oz plain flour (110 g)
2 oz butter (50 g)
a pinch of salt
iced water

Make a short crust with the flour, butter, a pinch of salt and enough iced water to make a soft dough. Roll into a ball and leave to rest for 2 hours.

Cook the pumpkin, cut into chunks, in the butter. When reduced almost to a purée add the sugar and the cream, then the prunes.

Roll out the pastry to fit a 7½ inch (18 cm) removable-base pie tin. Line the buttered and floured tin with the pastry. Put in the filling, strew with a little extra sugar. Bake in the centre of a fairly hot oven, gas mark 7 (450 °F, 230 °C) for 15 minutes, then at gas mark 5 (400 °F, 200 °C) for 20 to 25 minutes.

A variation is to use the flesh of a yellow or green honeydew melon instead of pumpkin. Melon doesn't reduce to a creamy purée as pumpkin does and you need only ¾ lb (350 g), so with one average sized melon two pies could be made.

Elizabeth David

Apple Tart

(Serves 8–12)

This is a recipe from Marseilles. It makes 2 x 7 inch tarts (2 x 18 cm).

1 lb eating apples (450 g)
8 oz rich shortcrust pastry (225 g)
4 tablespoons strawberry, raspberry or apricot jam
1 egg yolk

Make the pastry, roll it out as thinly as is sensible, and line two 7 or 8 inch flan tins (18 or 20 cm). Prick all over, sides too, with a fork.

Quarter, core and peel the apples and cut into very thin slices.

Mix the jam with a tablespoon or a little more of hot water so that you can spread it in a thick layer over the bottom of each tart. Lay the apple slices in a pattern on top of the jam; concentric circles is the most usual.

Beat the egg yolk and spread it over the top of the apples and the exposed sides of the pastry with your finger. (If you do not want to use an egg, use cream instead, and then sprinkle the tart lightly with sugar.) Bake in a pre-heated oven at gas mark 5 (375 °F, 190 °C) until cooked through and nicely gilded, about ½ an hour or even longer. A nearly-burned apple tart tastes and looks delicious.

This particular tart is *very* light and easy to make. Use leftover pastry to make a few jam turnovers to cook at the same time as the tart.

Caroline Conran.

Pear Caramel Roll

(Serves 4–6)

Quite irresistible. Spicy pears in a light moist crust with brown sugar and butter, all bubbled in the oven.

5 oz self-raising flour (150 g)
a pinch of salt
3 oz butter or block margarine (75 g)
¾ lb firm dessert pears (350 g)
1½ oz caster sugar (40 g)
2 level teaspoons finely grated orange rind
½ level teaspoon ground ginger
5 oz soft dark brown sugar (150 g)
2 oz butter or margarine (50 g)
1 tablespoon lemon juice

Sift flour and salt into a bowl. Rub in 3 oz fat (75 g). Add enough cold water to bind to a firm dough. Roll out on a floured surface to a rectangle 10 x 12 inches (25.5 x 30 cm). Peel and core the pears and grate over the dough. Sprinkle with the combined caster sugar, orange rind and ginger. Brush along edges of dough with cold water, roll up from one of the long sides and secure ends. Place in an ovenproof dish to fit tightly. Bake at gas mark 4 (350 °F, 180°C) for 15 minutes. Meanwhile, place the brown sugar, 2 oz fat (50 g) and lemon juice in a pan, stir over a low heat to dissolve. Simmer gently for 2 minutes. Pour over the roll and return to the oven for a further 25-30 minutes. Serve with or without pouring custard.

Margaret Coombes.

Plum Kuchen   (Serves 12)

This is a modern version of the fruited yeast cake that was made every Friday by Jewish housewives living in Austria and Hungary. This baking powder version is equally delicious, and much quicker to make.

For the batter:
8 oz self-raising flour (225 g) and 1 level teaspoon baking powder
or 8 oz plain flour (225 g), a pinch of salt and 3 level teaspoons baking powder
3 oz soft butter (75 g)
5 oz caster sugar (125 g)
1 egg
¼ pint milk (125 ml)

For the topping:
1 oz melted butter (25 g)
2 lb plums (weight before stoning) (1 kg)
6 oz granulated sugar (150 g)
1 level teaspoon cinnamon

Put all the batter ingredients into a bowl and beat by hand or machine until a thick, smooth batter is formed. This will take 2–3 minutes. The mixture is now ready to be used.

Spread the batter in an oiled tin, 12 x 9 x 2 inches (30 x 23 x 5 cm). Brush the batter with melted butter. Arrange the stoned and halved plums, flesh side up, all over the surface. Sprinkle with half the sugar. Bake in a quick moderate oven, gas mark 5 (375 °F, 190 °C) for 40 minutes, until well risen. Take out of the oven and sprinkle with the remaining 3 oz sugar (75 g). Allow to cool in the tin. Serve warm or cold, if possible with thick cream.

Evelyn Rose

Rhubarb Charlotte

(Serves 4)

1 lb rhubarb (450 g)
6 oz fresh white breadcrumbs (175 g)
2 oz melted butter (50 g)
2 oz brown sugar (50 g)
½ teaspoon ground ginger
¼ teaspoon each cinnamon and nutmeg
2 tablespoons golden syrup
1 tablespoon lemon juice

Toss the crumbs in the melted butter, then spread some of them in a thin layer at the bottom of a soufflé dish. Cover with the rhubarb cut into ½ inch lengths (1 cm).

Mix together the sugar and spices and sprinkle over the fruit. Repeat the layers till the dish is full, ending with a layer of crumbs.

Heat the syrup with the lemon juice and a couple of tablespoons of water. When melted, pour over the charlotte. Cover and bake in a moderate oven, gas mark 6 (400 °F, 200 °C) for 30 minutes; then uncover and cook for another 10 minutes or so, till the top is crisp and and golden.

If the rhubarb is very old and tough you may feel it is wise to give it a little preliminary steaming.

Margaret Costa

Tarte de Cambrai (Serves 6–8)
(Pear and Butter Cake)

A recipe given me in France—not in Cambrai, but in Montoire—which is foolproof and adaptable to other fruit.

3 large eating pears
lemon juice
10 level tablespoons self-raising flour
6 level tablespoons vanilla sugar
4 tablespoons oil or melted butter
8 tablespoons milk
2 whole eggs
a pinch of salt
2 oz butter (60 g)
sugar

Peel, core and slice the pears. Put them on a plate and sprinkle them with lemon juice—this prevents discolouration and improves their flavour. (If you are using hard windfall pears, cook them in a lemon flavoured syrup until just tender, then drain them well.)

Beat the next 6 ingredients together—an electric beater is ideal. Pour it into a greased tart or shallow cake tin, measuring

9½–10½ inches (24–27 cm). Arrange the pear slices on top. Dot with small bits of butter and sprinkle evenly with sugar. Bake at gas mark 6 (400 °F, 200 °C) until golden brown and crusted on top, and risen—takes from 35–50 minutes. Eat warm with cream, or cold as a cake.

Note: Eating apples, Cox's for instance, can be used instead of pears. Or drained, rinsed slices of canned peach: fresh peaches make too much juice to be suitable, unless you cook them first.

Jane Grigson

Cinnamon Apple
Pancakes
(Makes 8 pancakes)

For the batter:
4 oz flour (110 g)
¼ teaspoon salt
1 egg
½ pint milk or milk and water mixed (275 ml)
1 tablespoon salad oil

For the filling:
4 large Bramley apples, peeled, cored and sliced
¼ teaspoon ground cinnamon
6 oz demerara sugar (175 g)
6 oz butter (175 g)

Make the batter in the usual way and make about 8 pancakes using a 7 or 8 inch frying pan (18 or 20 cm). Stack the pancakes with a piece of greaseproof paper between each and set aside.

In a saucepan gently cook the apples, cinnamon, sugar and 4 oz butter (110 g), stirring occasionally, for about 20 minutes, or until the apples are tender. Spread the pancakes out on a flat surface, spoon some of the apple filling on to each and roll up.

In a large frying pan, melt the remaining butter. Fry the pancakes on all sides until golden brown, pile onto a warm serving dish and sprinkle them with more sugar and cinnamon. Serve hot with cream or ice cream.

Mary Berry

Clafoutis (Serves 6)

The texture of a clafoutis should be a cross between a custard and a pancake, soft but firm enough to unmould when cold. Traditionally it is made with black cherries but when those are out of season, a delicious clafoutis can be made with firm, tart eating apples, peeled, cored and thinly sliced.

3 level tablespoons plain flour
a pinch of salt
3 level tablespoons vanilla-flavoured caster sugar
2 eggs
1 tablespoon light olive oil
½ pint milk (275 ml)
1 lb black cherries, pitted (450 g)
butter
sifted icing sugar or caster sugar, to decorate

Sift the flour, salt and sugar into a bowl. Add the eggs and egg yolk, and work them together with a wooden spoon to make a smooth paste. Beat in the olive oil. Then gradually add the milk, beating vigorously to make a smooth, light batter. Put aside to rest while you prepare the fruit.

Pre-heat the oven to moderate, gas mark 4 (350 °F, 180 °C).

Generously butter a tart tin or ovenproof porcelain dish about 10 inches (25.5 cm) in diameter.

Spread the cherries (or apple slices) evenly in the dish and cover them with the batter, pouring it in over the back of a spoon to avoid disturbing them. Dot the top with a few tiny flakes of butter.

Bake clafoutis for 40 to 45 minutes, or until a knife blade slipped through to the bottom comes out clean. Dust with sifted icing sugar or caster sugar and serve warm. Alternatively, the clafoutis may be unmoulded, and there are some who like it cold.

Helena Radecho

Magdala Pancake (Serves 4)

To know this is to love it.

2 oz butter (50 g)
1½ oz caster sugar (40 g)
2 eggs
4 oz self-raising flour (110 g)
½ pint milk (275 ml)

Cream the butter and sugar thoroughly. Add the eggs and beat well. Sift the flour and fold in gently. Stir in the milk. Turn the mixture into a well-buttered baking dish and bake at gas mark 4 (350 °F, 180 °C) for 35 minutes. Four separate pancakes may be made in ovenproof saucers if preferred, but they will take a few minutes less to cook.

Harold Wilshaw

Chocolate Pudding

(Serves 4–6)

A rich, light pudding which isn't expensive to make. If you're short of time, turn the mixture into several individual moulds and steam them for about 45 minutes. Although a chocolate sauce would seem to be the perfect accompaniment, I find it's too heavy and suggest a little cream instead.

2 oz good plain chocolate (50 g)
3 oz butter (75 g)
3 oz caster sugar (75 g)
1 large egg
4 oz fresh white breadcrumbs (110 g)
2 oz self-raising flour (50 g)
milk to mix

Melt the chocolate in a small basin standing over a pan of hot water. Cream the butter and sugar until they are light and fluffy then beat in the chocolate. Separate the egg and beat the yolk into the chocolate mixture. Mix in the breadcrumbs (which should be very fine) with the flour, folding them in with 2 tablespoons of milk. Whisk the egg white stiffly and fold it carefully into the chocolate mixture, then turn it at once into a well-buttered charlotte mould. Cover the top with a piece of foil and steam the pudding for 1½ hours. If the centre seems at all soft when you look at the pudding, steam it for another 30 minutes. Serve with cream.

Kathie Webber

Chocolate Soufflé

(Serves 4)

This is a very rich, unctuous and dark chocolate soufflé, moister than the fluffier types. It only needs to have thick unsweetened pouring cream as an accompaniment.

3 oz dark chocolate (75 g)
¼ pint milk (150 ml)
2 oz caster sugar (50 g)
3 egg yolks
4 egg whites, stiffly beaten
1 teaspoon vanilla essence
1 level tablespoon cornflour
2 tablespoons thick cream

Cream together yolks, sugar, essence, cornflour and cream. In a heavy-bottomed pan melt the chocolate in the milk over a low heat, stirring from time to time. Combine the two mixtures in the pan and, stirring all the time, slowly bring to the boil; let the heat go from this before folding in 2 tablespoons of the beaten egg whites and incorporating these well. Deftly fold in the remainder of the egg whites and pour the mixture into a buttered soufflé dish.

Stand the dish on a hot metal tray in a pre-heated oven, gas mark 4 (350 °F, 180 °C). Bake for 40–50 minutes. Dredge the top with icing sugar before serving. Serve with hot chocolate sauce and/or whipped unsweetened cream.

Pineapple Alaska

(Serves 6)

One of my most exciting dishes. I found the art of producing this dramatic sweet purely by chance—you freeze it, meringue and all, before finishing if off in a hot oven just before serving it. Make the Alaska when pineapples are in season and reasonably priced and choose fruit that still has a green bloom to the stem.

1 medium pineapple
1 pint home made or bought ice cream (570 ml)
3 egg whites
3 oz caster sugar (75 g)

Prepare in advance. Remove and reserve the top of the pineapple. Remove the skin from the rest of the pineapple, gouging out any pips left in the fruit with a potato peeler or small spoon. Cut the pineapple into 6 slices removing the core from each slice. Reshape the pineapple on a fireproof serving dish, filling the core and masking the sides with ice cream, and place in the freezer.

Beat the egg white until stiff and lightly fold in the sugar. Smother the sides and top of the pineapple with the meringue, crown with the reserved top and freeze until 5 minutes before serving time.

Put the frozen dish into a hot oven, gas mark 6 (400 °F, 200 °C) and bake for 5 minutes or until the meringue is crispened and a light golden colour and serve at once, slicing sideways to give everyone one of the cut slices.

Marika Hanbury Tenison

Rich Rice Pudding

(Serves 6)

The inclusion of cream adds to the cost of this dish but parboiling the rice means you need less milk and shorter oven time than when making rice pudding by the traditional method. Praline, slices of banana, toasted nuts, grated chocolate, a few fresh blackberries or raspberries all make good alternative toppings to cinnamon sugar. Individual soufflé dishes in white fluted china are a best buy, I think. They look so pretty and are an ideal way of serving not-too-greedy portions of so many sweet and savoury foods from junket to mousses and first course salads such as courgettes à la grecque. I use them too as butter and pâté dishes, sugar bowls and containers for accompaniments to curries and kormas.

2 oz pudding rice (50 g)
¾ pint milk (425 ml)
2 tablespoons granulated sugar
1 teaspoon ground cinnamon
¼ pint double cream (150 ml)
3 tablespoons demerara sugar

Sprinkle the rice into a large pan of fast boiling water. Cook for 5 minutes, drain thoroughly and turn into an ovenproof dish. Bring the milk to scalding point. Remove from the heat, add the granulated sugar and ½ a teaspoon of cinnamon and stir until the sugar is dissolved. Pour over the rice, put a piece of greaseproof paper on top, cover with a lid and cook at gas mark 2 (300 °F, 150 °C), stirring occasionally. After 1–1¼ hours the rice should have absorbed the milk and become beautifully tender. When cold, whip the cream lightly, fold in the rice and divide between 6 small soufflé dishes. Cover and chill. Just before serving (no earlier or the topping will seep into the creamy rice) mix the brown sugar and remaining cinnamon together and sprinkle it on top of the puddings.

Philippa Davenport

Easter Pudding from
Mallorca (Pastel de Pascua) (Serves 4)

As a general rule the Spanish do not eat puddings as much as
we do in Britain. They prefer to end a meal with cheese and fruit.
This is an exception, however, and is both economical and
nutritious. It is made especially for Easter Monday by the
country people of Mallorca.

1¾ pints milk (1 litre)
9 oz sugar (225 g)
grated rind of 1 orange and 2 lemons
1 stick cinnamon (or 1 teaspoon ground cinnamon)
4 eggs
2 oz semi-sweet biscuit crumbs (crushed digestive biscuits are good
for this) (50 g)

Put the milk in a large saucepan, add the sugar, orange and
lemon rind and cinnamon and bring to the boil. Allow to cool
while you whisk the eggs until they are light and frothy. When
the milk is cool, remove the cinnamon stick and fold in the
beaten eggs. Carefully stir in the crushed biscuits and pour into
a large well-buttered ovenproof dish. Put into a fairly hot oven,
gas mark 5 (375 °F, 190 °C) and bake for about an hour until
slightly risen and golden. Serve cold.

Anna Macmiaidhachain

Strawberries in Orange Cream

(Serves 4)

A mouthwatering way to serve strawberries, especially if you haven't got quite enough to go round.

1 lb strawberries (450 g)
8 fl oz double cream (225 ml)
2–3 tablespoons caster sugar
1 small carton plain yoghurt
grated rind and juice of 1 small orange

Take the stalks off the strawberries and halve them if they are large. In a large bowl whip the cream until thick and then stir in the sugar, the yoghurt and then gradually the orange rind and juice. Lightly stir in the strawberries and transfer the mixture to a pretty glass bowl if possible. Chill in the fridge before serving.

Josceline Dimbleby

Oranges with Honey, Almonds and Rosewater (Serves 4)

Sugar is something which I try to restrict as much as possible in my cooking because I don't think it is good from a health point of view. However, my family don't consider they've had a good meal unless it ends with something sweet, so I've developed a repertoire of puddings which make use of the natural sugar in fresh and dried fruit, together with a little honey. This recipe is a typical example.

6 large or 8 medium oranges
3 tablespoons clear honey
1 tablespoon rosewater
2 oz flaked almonds (50 g)

Using a sharp knife, cut the peel and pith from the oranges, then cut the orange flesh into pieces and put into a bowl, discarding the white membrane. Add the honey to the oranges, together with the rosewater. Mix well, then chill. Meanwhile toast the almonds in a dry grill pan under a moderate heat until golden. Serve the oranges in small glass bowls with the golden crunchy almonds scattered on top.

Rose Elliot

Pears in Cider

(Serves 6)

Pears for cooking should be as hard as you can get them—then they'll retain their shape and texture for this delicious pudding with a coating of lovely cider syrup.

6 large, hard pears
1 pint dry cider
4 oz sugar (110 g)
2 whole cinnamon sticks
1 vanilla pod
1 level dessertspoon arrowroot
toasted flaked almonds
¼ pint double cream (150 ml)

Pre-heat the oven to gas mark ½ (250 °F, 130 °C).

Peel the pears carefully, leaving the stalks on, and lay them in a large casserole. Then in a saucepan bring the cider, cinnamon and sugar to the boil, add the vanilla pod, and pour the whole lot over the pears. Cover the casserole and put it into the oven for the pears to bake very slowly for about 3 hours. (Half way through the cooking time turn them over.)

When the time is up transfer them to a bowl to cool, and pour the liquid back into the saucepan—discarding the vanilla pod and the cinnamon sticks. In a cup mix a dessertspoon of arrowroot to a smooth paste with a little cold water, then add that to the saucepan. Bring to the boil, stirring until the mixture has thickened slightly and become syrupy. Then pour it over the pears, allow to cool and baste to give each pear a good coating of syrup. Pop them into the refrigerator to chill thoroughly, and serve sprinkled with toasted flaked almonds and thick whipped cream.

Chilled Chocolate Cake

This rich, unusual gâteau isn't baked—it's frozen. The basis of this mixture is almost any kind of cake or sweet biscuit crumbs—Madeira, Victoria sandwich, trifle sponges; anything except fruit cake. Crumble stale cake, or crush it with a rolling pin. Serve this cake as a dessert after a simple main course.

1 lb cake and/or biscuit crumbs (450 g)
4 oz ground almonds (110 g)
2 oz glacé cherries, halved (50 g)
2 oz walnuts, chopped (50 g)
2 oz plain chocolate, melted (50 g)
6 tablespoons pineapple jam
1 tablespoon brandy

For the decoration:
12 oz plain chocolate (350 g)
8 oz butter or margarine (225 g)
1 lb icing sugar (450 g)
2 oz cocoa, dissolved in about 1 tablespoon hot water (50 g)
gravy browning
1 oz chocolate, grated (25 g)
6 glacé cherries
a few pieces of crystallised ginger

Put the crumbs in a large basin and mix in the almonds, cherries, walnuts, and melted chocolate. Melt the jam in a saucepan; mix with the crumb mixture and brandy to give a fairly sticky mixture. Spoon into a greased, lined, 7 inch (18 cm) loose bottomed cake tin. Press well down and leave for 1 hour in the freezer or 2 hours in a refrigerator. Remove from the tin.

To decorate, melt 8 oz chocolate (225 g) in a basin over hot water. Pour over cake to coat evenly. Allow to set. Make butter icing with the icing sugar, butter, 4 oz melted chocolate (110 g) and the cocoa. Put ⅓ of the icing into a separate bowl; add enough gravy browning to make a dark brown icing. With a small star nozzle, pipe the dark icing round the base, top edge and sides of the cake. With a large star nozzle, pipe an overlapping rope design in the paler icing, leaving room for grated chocolate. Decorate with cherries and ginger.

Alex Baker

Cakes, Biscuits and Bread

Carrot and Walnut Cake (Makes 15 pieces)

For the cake:
6 oz soft brown sugar (175 g)
7 fl oz tasteless vegetable oil (200 ml)
2 standard eggs, beaten
8 oz plain flour (225 g), sifted with
1 level teaspoon bicarbonate of soda and
1 teaspoon cinnamon
6 oz coarsely grated carrots (175 g) (i.e. about 3 medium carrots,
    topped, tailed and peeled)
4 oz walnut pieces, chopped (110 g)

For the topping:
4 oz full fat soft cream cheese (110 g)
2 oz unsalted butter (50 g)
2 oz icing sugar, sieved (50 g)

Brush a tin 11 x 7 x 1½ inches (28 x 18 x 4 cm) with melted fat. Line the base with greaseproof paper, and brush the paper as well. Pre-heat the oven to gas mark 2 (300 °F, 150°C).

The cake is simplicity itself to make; just beat the ingredients together, one after the other in the order in which they are given in the recipe. Spread the mixture in the prepared tin and bake in the centre of the oven for 40 minutes or until the cake is nicely risen, firm to the touch and has begun to shrink away slightly from the sides of the tin. Leave to cool in the tin and when only just warm turn it out onto a wire rack.

The topping is just as simple as the cake is to make! Beat all the ingredients together until the mixture is smooth then spread over the top of the cooled cake. Leave in a cool place to firm up a little before dividing into 15 sections and serving.

Caroline Liddell

Mixed Fruit and Pineapple Cake

(Serves 10)

2 oz glacé cherries (50 g)
7 oz self-raising flour (200 g)
1 lb can of pineapple chunks, rings or crushed, excluding the juice
(450 g)
5 oz butter (150 g)
4½ oz soft brown sugar (125 g)
2 large eggs, beaten
2 tablespoons milk
12 oz mixed dried fruit (350 g)

Grease an 8 inch round cake tin (20 cm) and line with greaseproof paper. Pre-heat the oven to gas mark 3 (325 °F, 170 °C).

Cut the cherries into halves and roll in flour. Drain and chop the pineapple very finely. Cream the butter and sugar together until light and creamy. Beat in the eggs, adding a tablespoon of flour with the last amount of egg. Fold in the flour, milk and last of all the fruit, including the pineapple. Turn into the prepared tin, place in the centre of the oven and bake for about 2 hours or until pale golden, shrinking away from the sides of the tin. Leave to cool in the tin, remove the paper and store in a plastic container in the refrigerator as this is a very moist cake.

Note: Because canned pineapple is added to this fruit cake, it needs special care in storage. Keep it wrapped or in a container in the refrigerator for up to 2 months. It is a beautifully moist and a very special cake. A larger version could be used as a lighter coloured Christmas fruit cake.

Mary Berry.

Jamaican Gâteau

This is not based on a Caribbean dish but a simply splendid way of turning a very ordinary sponge into a super gâteau by using ingredients associated with Jamaica.

For the sponge cake:
6 oz butter (175 g)
6 oz caster sugar (175 g)
3 large eggs
6 oz self-raising flour (175 g)

For the filling:
2 heaped tablespoons ground coffee
just over ½ pint water (300 ml)
a miniature bottle of rum
3 oz butter (75 g)
5 oz icing sugar (125 g)
1 oz cocoa (25 g) or 2 oz chocolate powder (50 g)

For the decorations:
½ pint double cream (300 ml)
1 oz icing sugar (25 g)
about 12 finger shaped meringues (see below)
2 oz plain chocolate (50 g)

To make the sponge cake cream the butter and sugar until soft and light then gradually blend in the beaten eggs and fold in the sieved flour. Put into a greased and floured 7–8 inch cake tin (18–20 cm) and bake in the centre of a moderate oven, gas mark 3–4 (325 °–350 °F, 160 °–180 °C) until firm to the touch. Allow to cool, then cut into four layers. Put a round of greaseproof paper into the cake tin, then a layer of sponge.

For the filling: make the coffee in your favourite way with the water. It will be very strong because you are using only ½ pint water (300 ml) to a generous amount of coffee. Blend in some of the rum. Prepare the chocolate flavoured butter icing by creaming the butter, icing sugar and cocoa or chocolate powder. Moisten the first layer of sponge in the tin with about ¼ of the liquid coffee, then cover with ⅓ of the chocolate butter icing. Repeat this until all the layers of cake are back in the tin, and spoon the remaining coffee over the top layer. Put a round of greaseproof paper over the cake and a light weight. Leave for about 24 hours. Turn out on to a serving dish. Whip the cream until it just begins to hold its shape, then blend in the sieved icing sugar and then the remainder of the rum. Spread over the top and sides of the cake. Decorate the sides with small finger shaped meringues and grate the chocolate over the top of the cake.

To make the meringues: whisk 2 egg whites until stiff; gradually whisk in 2 oz caster sugar (50 g). Grease a baking tray with a very little butter or olive oil and pipe the meringues on this. Dry out in a cool oven, gas mark 0–½, (200 °–225 °F, 90°–110 °C) for 1½–2 hours until quite firm.

My Mother's Chocolate Cake

(Serves 10)

The joy of this cake is that it remains moist for a long time, not that anyone allows it to remain very long because it is ambrosia. You can freeze it and the frosting separately.

For the cake:
8 oz sifted plain flour (225 g)
3 teaspoons baking powder
¼ teaspoon bicarbonate of soda
4 oz butter (125 g)
3 oz caster sugar (75 g)
3 egg yolks
8 oz plain chocolate, melted (225 g)
½ pint milk (300 ml)
¼ teaspoon vanilla essence
3 egg whites

For the fudge frosting:
5½ oz plain chocolate (Bournville) (165 g)
½ pint milk (300 ml)
1¼ lb caster sugar (560 g)
2 oz butter (50 g)
2 teaspoons vanilla essence

Pre-heat the oven to gas mark 4 (350 °F, 180 °C).
   Sift the flour and baking powder separately and mix. Add the bicarbonate of soda and salt, and sift together twice more. Cream the butter thoroughly, add the sugar gradually. Cream until light and fluffy. Beat the egg yolks until light. Add them to the butter and sugar and then add the melted chocolate. Next add the flour mixture, alternating a little at a time with the milk. Beat until smooth. Add the vanilla essence and fold in the beaten egg whites. Pour the batter into two 8 x 2½ inch (20 x 6 cm) cake pans and bake in the pre-heated oven for 30 minutes, or until a skewer inserted in the middle comes out clean. Cool

on cake racks. When cool split the layers horizontally to make a 4-layer cake. Spread fudge frosting between each layer and over the top of the cake.

To make the frosting: melt the chocolate, add the milk and sugar. Boil until the mixture forms a ball when dropped into cold water. Add the butter and vanilla essence. Let stand, then beat until cool. If the frosting is too thick to spread easily, add milk until a spreading consistency is obtained. For decorating cakes, add icing sugar until it is sufficiently thick.

Chocolate Beer Cake (Serves 8)

For the cake:
butter
plain flour
2 oz bitter dessert chocolate (50 g)
¼ level teaspoon salt
1 level teaspoon baking powder
¼ level teaspoon bicarbonate of soda
6 oz caster sugar (175 g)
2 eggs
8 fl oz lager (225 ml)
3 oz walnuts, coarsely chopped (optional) (75 g)

For the filling:
2 oz softened butter (50 g)
4 oz icing sugar, sifted (100 g)
1–2 tablespoons lager (taken from the 8 fl oz)
2 oz bitter dessert chocolate, melted and cooled (50 g)

Butter 2 x 8 inch sandwich tins (20 cm) and dust lightly with flour. Pre-heat the oven to moderate, gas mark 4 (350 °F, 180 °C).

Melt the dessert chocolate in the top of a double saucepan and allow to cool to lukewarm. Sift 8 oz flour (225 g), the salt, baking powder and bicarbonate of soda into a bowl. In another bowl, cream 4 oz butter (100 g); add the sugar gradually and beat until light and fluffy. Beat in the eggs, one at a time, followed by the melted chocolate. Then add the flour mixture gradually, alternating it with lager (save 1 or 2 tablespoons for the filling) and beating vigorously until the batter is well blended. Fold in the walnuts, if used.

Pour the batter into the prepared tins and bake for 25–30 minutes, or until the layers spring back when pressed lightly with the finger. Remove tins from oven; allow to cool for 5 minutes, then turn the layers out on wire racks and leave to become quite cold.

To make the filling: cream the softened butter with the icing sugar until very light. Add the lager and lukewarm melted chocolate and beat vigorously until well blended. Chill until firm before using.

Sandwich the cake layers with chocolate filling and spread the remainder over the top and sides. (If you have not included nuts in the batter, you can decorate the top of the cake with walnut halves.)

Express Chocolate Cake (Serves 8)

6½ oz plain flour (185 g)
2 tablespoons cocoa
1 level teaspoon bicarbonate of soda
1 level teaspoon baking powder
5 oz caster sugar (150 g)
2 tablespoons golden syrup
2 eggs, lightly beaten
¼ pint salad or corn oil (150 ml)
¼ pint milk (150 ml)

For the filling and icing:
¼ pint whipping cream (150 ml)
apricot jam
3 oz plain chocolate (75 g)
grated chocolate or chocolate curls

Pre-heat the oven to gas mark 3 (325 °F, 170 °C).

Sieve the flour, cocoa, bicarbonate of soda and baking powder into a large mixing bowl. Make a well in the centre and add the syrup and sugar. Gradually stir in the eggs, oil and milk and beat well to make a smooth batter.

Pour into two greased and lined 8 inch sandwich tins (20 cm) and bake for 30–35 minutes, or until the cakes spring back when lightly pressed with a fingertip. Turn out onto a wire rack and leave to cool.

Whip the cream until it will stand in soft peaks. Sandwich the cakes together with the cream and apricot jam. Melt the chocolate gently on a plate over a pan of hot water. Do not stir or it will harden. Spread it over the top of the cake. Decorate the edge with grated plain or milk chocolate or curls.

Mary Berry.

Rock Buns (Makes 18)

Being convinced of the value of wholefoods, I use either 100 per cent or 81 per cent wholewheat flour for all my cooking, together with (usually) barbados muscovado sugar. Obviously the resulting texture and flavour are not the same as those achieved with white flour and sugar—but cakes and cookies made with these unrefined ingredients have their own wholesome charm and natural flavour. The wholewheat flour seems to work particularly well in these buns which I find are always popular. They're also quick and easy to make.

8 oz 100 per cent wholewheat plain flour (225 g)
2 teaspoons baking powder
1 teaspoon mixed spice
4 oz butter, cut into rough pieces (125 g)
4 oz barbados muscovado sugar (125 g)
4 oz mixed dried fruit (125 g)
2 oz candied peel, chopped (50 g)
1 egg, beaten

Pre-heat the oven to gas mark 8 (450 °F, 230 °C). Lightly grease a large baking sheet.

Sift the flour, baking powder and spice into a large bowl; there will be a little residue of bran left behind in the sieve—add this to the rest of the flour in the bowl. Using your finger tips rub the butter into the mixture until it resembles fine breadcrumbs, then stir in the sugar, dried fruit and peel. Add the egg, stirring lightly with a fork so that the mixture just holds together. It is very important that it is not too wet or the buns will be rock-like in more ways than one.

Put rough heaps of the mixture on to the prepared baking sheet—again, don't press them together too much. Bake in the pre-heated oven for 12–15 minutes, until set and lightly browned. Cool on a wire rack.

Rose Elliot

Currant Squares

In the pages of *Woman's Weekly* magazine we called this type of recipe a traybake as it is cooked in a swiss roll tin, then cut into pieces to be served. Make a note of the pastry mix—it's very quick and easy to prepare and can be used for all types of pies and tartlets.

For the pastry:
12 oz plain flour (350 g)
10 oz margarine, in a hard block straight from a cold place (275 g)
a pinch of salt
a little caster sugar

For the filling:
2 oz butter or margarine (50 g)
2 oz soft brown sugar (50 g)
1 oz chopped mixed peel (25 g)
8 oz cleaned currants (225 g)

Sift the flour and salt together, and using a coarse grater, grate the margarine straight into the flour and mix it well with a knife. Stir in sufficient cold water to make a soft but not sticky dough, similar in texture to short crust pastry. Wrap the dough in greaseproof paper and leave it in a cool place for 15 minutes to rest.

Next make the filling. Put the butter and sugar into a pan and over a gentle heat melt them together then stir in the currants and mixed peel.

Using half the pastry, line the base and sides of a swiss roll tin measuring 8 x 12 inches (20 x 30 cm). Then spread it evenly with the fruit filling. Roll the rest of the pastry large enough to cover the surface. Moisten the edges of the pastry in the tin then lift the top into place and press it firmly to the pastry below. Trim the edges. Score the surface into small diamonds with the point for a knife, brush with water and sprinkle thickly with caster sugar.

Bake the traybake on the centre shelf of a hot oven, gas mark 8 (450 °F, 230 °C) for 20 minutes then reduce the heat to gas mark 6 (400 °F, 200 °C) for a further 10 to 15 minutes or until the pastry is golden brown and cooked. Leave the Currant Squares in the tin to cool then cut them into pieces before serving for tea.

Janet Warren

A Groppi

For some time during the war I was a prisoner, and I must say it concentrated the mind wonderfully upon food. I thought it might be of interest to set down one of the recipes on which we sustained ourselves. A Groppi was a great treat, and only possible when we had received a Canadian Red Cross parcel, which contained real butter, arrowroot biscuits and a dried milk called Klim which, mixed with only a little water made a passable 'cream'.

arrowroot biscuits
butter
jam
cream

For each Groppi (so called nostalgically after the famous pastrycooks in Cairo), soak two arrowroot biscuits in water until they are quite soft but not disintegrating. Fry these golden brown in butter, spread one with jam and sandwich it, spread the top with jam, and cover with cream.

Harold Wilshaw

Nig Nogs

(Makes 20)

Crisp and crunchy . . . gorgeous home made cookies can be quite irresistible, sparring with any rich gooey extravagant gâteau. And not just for elevenses, four o'clock tea or a bedtime send off. They'll fill an energy gap and soften up the plumber. A big batch makes you Brown Owl's favourite mother. Start baking!

3 oz plain flour (75 g)
½ level teaspoon bicarbonate of soda
3 oz caster sugar (75 g)
3 oz rolled oats (75 g)
3 oz butter or margarine (75 g)
1 tablespoon milk
1 tablespoon golden syrup

Sift the flour and bicarbonate of soda into a bowl, stir in the sugar and oats. Warm the butter, milk and syrup together in a pan until melted but not bubbling. Stir into the dry ingredients and mix well. Roll into small balls and place well apart on greased baking sheets. Flatten slightly and bake in the oven at gas mark 2 (300 °F, 150 °C) for about 25 minutes until golden brown. Cool on the sheets for a minute or two then transfer the cookies to a wire rack to cool completely, using a palette knife slipped under to ease them away.

Margaret Coombes.

Coconut Wafers (Makes about 16)

Crisp and wafer-thin, these store well in an airtight tin. They are handy as a crunchy partner to soft textured fruit desserts and ice cream as well as with tea, coffee or chocolate.

2 oz butter (50 g)
2 oz caster sugar (50 g)
1 level tablespoon golden syrup
2 teaspoons lemon juice
2 oz plain flour (50 g)
1 oz dessicated coconut, very finely chopped (25 g)

Cream together the butter and sugar until light and fluffy. Beat in the syrup. Fold in the lemon juice, flour and coconut and mix well. Place 1 teaspoonful at a time on a greased baking sheet, keeping them well apart as the wafers spread. Bake at gas mark 4 (350 °F, 180 °C) for about 15 minutes, when the edges should be golden brown and the centre lightly coloured. Cool slightly before lifting carefully from the tray with a palette knife onto a wire rack.

Margaret Coombes.

Fruit Tea Bread

(Makes 1 large loaf)

Teabreads are marvellous for weekends and for picnics when you can serve them sliced and buttered. In this traditional recipe the dried fruit and sugar are soaked overnight in cold tea so that the fruit plumps up and softens to produce a fruit bread that is moist and delicious to eat.

10 oz mixed dried fruit (275 g)
7 oz soft brown sugar (200 g)
½ pint strained cold tea (275 ml)
1 egg
10 oz self-raising flour (275 g)

Measure the dried fruit and soft brown sugar into a mixing basin. Pour over the cold tea and leave to stand overnight. Next day stir up the ingredients, add the egg and flour and mix thoroughly.

Pour the mixture into a well buttered 9 x 5 x 3 inch large loaf pan (23 x 13 x 7.5 cm) and bake in the centre of a moderate oven, gas mark 4 (350 °F, 180 °C) for 1½ hours. Loosen sides, turn out and allow to cool.

Katie Stewart

Sesame Bread

(Makes 1 loaf)

A well-baked, tasty loaf and a crunchy salad make the perfect lunch without any need for the main protein foods such as cheese or meat. This loaf is nutty and substantial and goes well with savoury vegetables and with honey.

8 oz wholemeal flour (225 g)
1 teaspoon fine sea salt
2 tablespoons sesame seeds
¾ oz fresh yeast or ½ oz dried (15 g or 10 g)
1 teaspoon honey
3 fl oz warm water (75 ml)
1 egg, beaten
1 tablespoon tahini (a paste made of crushed or ground sesame seeds, rather like peanut butter only more bitter and available from most wholefood stores)

Put the flour into a bowl with the salt and sesame seeds. Cream the yeast with the honey, mix in the water and set them in a warm place for the yeast to froth. Make a well in the centre of the flour and pour in the yeast mixture. Add the egg and tahini and mix everything to a dough. Turn it out on to a floured board and knead it well (it should be fairly stiff).

Return the dough to the bowl, cover it with a clean tea cloth and leave it in a warm place for 1 hour to rise.

Heat the oven to gas mark 6 (400 °F, 200 °C). Knead the dough again and shape it into a round. Set it on a floured baking sheet, cover it with the cloth again and put it on top of the stove for 30 minutes to prove. Bake the loaf for 35 minutes and then cool it on a wire rack.

It will rise more when it proves than it does in the initial rising. It bakes to a rich brown and as it cools it develops a thin but crispy crust. It is light textured and nutty and best with saltless butter, but strangely enough goes beautifully with Marmite as well.

209

Beer Bread

This bread never fails, and is the ideal recipe for cooks unfamiliar with, or not good at, yeast cookery. It comes from Leith's School of Food and Wine's Beginner's Course.

½ lb wholewheat flour (225 g)
½ lb plain white flour (225 g)
½ pint brown ale (275 ml)
1 oz fresh yeast (25 g)
1 heaped tablespoon soft brown sugar
1 level teaspoon salt
1 egg
2 oz butter (50 g)

Use a little of the butter to brush out a 2 lb loaf tin (900 g).

Bring the sugar, beer and the rest of the butter to boiling point and then allow to cool until lukewarm. Use a spoon or two of this liquid to cream the yeast. Add creamed yeast, salt and lightly beaten egg to the beer mixture.

Warm a large mixing bowl and sift the flour into it. Make a well in the centre and pour in the liquid. Mix, first with a knife, and then with your fingers, to a soft but not sloppy dough. Knead for 10 minutes or until smooth and a little shiny. It should be very elastic.

Put the dough back in the bowl and cover it with a piece of greased polythene. Put in a warm place until it has doubled in bulk.

Take out and punch down and knead until smooth again. Shape the dough into a loaf shape and put into the tin. Cover with the greased polythene again and put back in the warm place to prove (rise again to double its bulk). It should now look the shape of the finished loaf.

While it is proving pre-heat the oven to gas mark 5 (375 °F, 190 °C). Bake the load in the middle of the oven for 35 minutes or until it is brown on top and the bread sounds hollow when tapped on the underside. Cool, tipped out on a wire rack.

Prudence Leith.

Potato Rolls

(Makes 8 large or 16 small)

An unusual bread roll, these are excellent served with butter to accompany salads, soups, or creamy fish or chicken dishes. Also good with a plain cheese.

¼ oz fresh yeast (5 g)
1½ oz sugar (40 g)
4 fl oz milk (110 ml)
3 oz butter (75 g)
2 teaspoons sea salt
1 egg
3 oz freshly mashed potato (75 g)
¾ lb white flour (350 g)

Put the yeast in a cup with 1 teaspoon sugar and 2 fl oz luke warm water (55 ml). Put in a warm place for 10 minutes. Put two large mixing bowls also in the warm. Heat the milk until luke warm, and add the butter cut in pieces, off the heat. When the yeast starts to bubble, pour it into a large bowl and add the milk and semi-melted butter. Stir well with a wooden spoon, adding the rest of the sugar, the salt, and the beaten egg. Stir until blended, then beat into the hot mashed potato, in the second bowl. When amalgamated, start to stir in the flour, a cup at a time. When the dough starts to cling together turn out onto a floured board and start kneading, adding the remaining flour as needed, until it is smooth and springy. Knead for 6–8 minutes, then put in a clean buttered bowl, turning over to coat with fat. Cover with a cling-film wrap or a thick cloth, and leave in a warm place for 2 hours, till roughly doubled in size. Punch down, turn out and knead lightly for another 5 minutes. Then shape into round rolls and lay on a greased baking sheet, or in round tins. It will make 8 large rolls or 16 small ones. Replace the rolls in a warm place for 30 minutes to rise again, then bake at gas mark 5 (375 °F, 190 °C). Large rolls will take about 25 minutes; small ones 20 minutes. Test by knocking with a knuckle to see if they give the right hollow sound. Cool briefly on a wire rack, and eat while still warm, or cool completely and re-warm slightly before serving.

Arabella Boxer.

Preserves
Pickles and Chutneys

Spiced Cherry Jam (Makes 4½ lb) (about 2 kg)

I make this delectable jam from garden morellos, but it is equally good with any tart cherry.

2 lb morello (sour red) or other tart red cherries (1 kg)
juice of 1 large lemon
3¼ lb granulated sugar (1.5 kg)
½ level teaspoon ground cinnamon
½ level teaspoon mixed spice
½ bottle liquid pectin (4 fl oz) (100 ml)

Wash jam jars thoroughly, then put in a low oven, gas mark 1 (275 °F, 140 °C) to dry and warm whilst making jam.

Half fill the blender with stoned cherries and blend for a few seconds or chop cherries by hand. In preserving pan, put the cherries (and any juice which comes out when they are stoned), lemon juice, sugar and spice and heat until the sugar is dissolved, stirring all the time. Bring to a full rolling boil, then boil for one minute, stirring constantly. Add the half bottle of pectin off the heat. Continue to stir for 5 minutes to distribute fruit and skim if necessary. Pour into hot jars and cover with waxed discs. Cover with cellophane or foil when cold.

Evelyn Rose

Orange and Ginger
Marmalade (Makes 8–10 lb) (3.5–4.5 kg)

To any traditional marmalade recipe you can add the flavour of ginger simply by simmering root ginger with the fruit peel and stirring in chopped crystallised ginger just before potting. Buy root ginger from a chemist—one specialising in home wine making will certainly stock it.

3 lb bitter oranges (1.35 kg)
1 oz root ginger (25 g)
6 pints water (3.4 litres)
juice of 2 lemons
6 lb granulated sugar (2.7 kg)
2 oz crystallised ginger (50 g)

Scrub the oranges and pick off the discs at the stalk end. Cut in half, squeeze out the juice and reserve. Pull away pulp and pith from inside the orange halves, then quarter the peels and shred them finely. Cut up the pulp and pith roughly and tie in a muslin bag with the pips and the bruised root ginger—give the ginger a hearty whack with a rolling pin to crack and 'bruise' the surface, which releases the flavour.

Place the shredded orange peel, the muslin bag of pith and pips and the water into a preserving pan. Bring to the boil, then simmer gently for about 2 hours or until the peel feels quite soft and tender when squeezed between the fingers. Draw the pan off the heat. Squeeze the muslin bag by pressing between two dinner plates to extract all the juice, and discard.

Add the sugar and stir over a low heat until the sugar has dissolved. Then bring to a boil and cook briskly for a set—takes 15–20 minutes. Draw off the heat and skim. Wash the sugary coating off the crystallised ginger and chop the ginger finely. Add to the pan of marmalade and then allow the marmalade to cool for about 15 minutes, or until a thin skin begins to form on the surface. Stir once and pour into warm dry jars. Cover with waxed circles and leave until cold before sealing with cellophane covers.

Katie Stewart.

Quince Jelly

The best of all jellies. Serve it with Jockey fromage frais or curd cheese whipped with a little cream and sugar, or with bread and butter, or with lamb, pork, duck, game, etcetera.

3 fine quinces
6 lb quinces and apples (3 kg) in the best proportions you can manage,
    from 3 lb of each (1½ kg) to 1½ lb quinces (¾ kg) with
    apples to make up the weight
water
sugar

Peel, core and cut the 3 quinces into dice. Simmer them in a covered pan with 2 pints water (1.2 litres) until tender. Reserve the dice and their liquid. Put their debris into a large pan with the 6 lb fruit (3 kg) cut into rough ¾ inch pieces (2 cm), skin, core and all. Pour on 4 pints of water (2.4 litres), then the strained liquor from cooking the quince pieces which should be set aside for the moment. Bring to simmering point, cover and cook for up to 1½ hours, until the fruit is soft and disintegrating. Strain it off through a jelly bag. Add the quince dice and measure. To each pint (600 ml) allow 1 lb sugar (500 g). Bring juice and dice to the boil and stir in the sugar. Bring back to the boil and boil hard until setting point is reached. Leave the pan to cool down, as you do with marmalade, so that the dice remain evenly distributed, then pot in the usual way.

217

marmalade, so that the dice remain evenly distributed, then pot in the usual way.

Don't waste the fruit pulp; quinces are too precious to be thrown away until they have yielded the last of their flavour. Cover it with water generously, and simmer for another hour. Sieve it, so that you get some of the pulp with the juice, then boil it with sugar as above, to make a homely preserve half way between a jelly and a fruit butter. Good on bread and butter, or with pork instead of apple sauce.

Jane Grigson

Lemon Curd

(Makes 2 lb) (900 g)

3 lemons
½ lb granulated sugar (225 g)
2–3 eggs
4 oz butter (110 g)

Pare the rind from the lemons very thinly. Squeeze the juice from the lemons and strain it. Melt the butter, add sugar, lemon juice, lemon peel and beaten eggs, mix and thicken gently in the top half of a double boiler, or in a stone jar such as a Keillers Oxford Marmalade jar standing in a pan of water.

Stir constantly until it coats the back of the spoon. Strain through a wire strainer. Bottle in hot sterilised jars. It keeps, in the refrigerator, for a week or two.

Caroline Conran.

Dukka

I make lots of this every autumn when hedgerows are rich with cob and hazelnuts. It keeps well for many months if stored in an airtight jar. The quantity given here neatly fills a 1 lb Kilner jar (450 g). To eat dukka, break off pieces of crusty hot bread, moisten with olive oil and dip into the nutty mixture. Served with a vegetable purée soup I think this makes a perfect lunch.

4 oz hazelnut kernels (110 g)
2 oz sesame seeds (50 g)
1 oz coriander seeds (25 g)
1 teaspoon cumin seeds
salt

Place a small frying pan (no fat) over the fire. When hot add the hazelnuts and cook, stirring and turning, until the skins begin to blacken and peel away. Empty the pan and toast the sesame seeds. Empty the pan again and toast the coriander and cumin together. Mix the ingredients and crush them to a very coarse powder using a mincer or coffee grinder. Season to taste with salt.

Philippa Davenport

Pickled Plums

5 lb rather under-ripe plums (2.5 kg)
5 lb sugar (2.5 kg)
1½ pints wine vinegar (1 litre)
a stick of cinnamon
cloves

Prepare a syrup by boiling the sugar and vinegar together for a few minutes; add the cinnamon and 2 tablespoons of whole cloves. After a few minutes boiling put in the plums, which should have been jabbed here and there with a small skewer. Bring to the boil again, remove the scum, and take out the plums at once. Put them in a large bowl. Boil the syrup for another 3 or 4 minutes, pour over the plums. Leave in a cold place for 24 hours, and then repeat the boiling process; i.e. strain off the syrup, bring it to the boil, put in the plums, boil them half a minute, remove them, continue to boil the syrup a minute or two, pour over the plums. Next day the pickle can be put into bottles or jars and sealed. Leave for six weeks before opening.

Elizabeth David

Pickled Mushrooms

1 lb small young mushrooms (450 g)
vinegar
2 blades of mace
½ level teaspoon white pepper
1 level teaspoon ground ginger
¼ onion, chopped

Remove stalks and peel mushrooms. Place in a pan and cover with vinegar. Add the remaining ingredients. Cook gently until tender, pack and pour in the liquid. Lid and store.

Alex Barker

Lemons in Oil

24 lemons
salt
chilli powder
¼ pint olive oil (150 ml)

Wash and dry lemons, cut into thin wedges or slices. Layer in jars, sprinkling each layer with salt and chilli. Top up with oil. Lid and store for at least 2–3 weeks.

Alex Barber

Marrow Mangoes

At the beginning of the 18th century, sailors of the East India Company started to bring back a range of fruit and vegetables previously unknown in England, and among the list were mangoes. English cooks soon devised ways of imitating these, and this recipe is one that has survived.

a small vegetable marrow, about 2–3 lb (1–1.5 kg)
malt vinegar
sugar—4 oz for each 1 pint of vinegar (100 g for 600 ml)
2 onions, chopped
1 teaspoon grated horseradish
2 teaspoons white mustard seed
4 pieces root ginger
2 tablespoons black peppercorns

Peel the marrow, cut it in half lengthways and scoop out the seeds. Then put it to soak overnight in salt water. The next day prepare the filling by mixing together the onion, horseradish, mustard seed, root ginger and peppercorns. (It's difficult to give exact quantities here, as so much depends on the shape and size of the marrow, how much you have hollowed it out and how fiery you want the pickle to be. But the mixture given above should be a useful guide.) When you have the mixture ready, drain the marrow and pack the seed space with the filling. Tie the two halves together with string. You will probably need to secure the marrow with about 3 pieces of string along its length otherwise too much of the filling will escape. Then put the marrow into a large stone jar or crock and cover it with a boiling solution of vinegar. Put a cloth over the crock to keep out flies.

Next day drain off the vinegar and reboil. This should be repeated every day until the marrow looks dark and soft (it usually takes about 10 days). Don't worry if a little of the spice mixture does escape during handling and steeping; in fact this helps to spice the vinegar. When the marrow is ready, take it out of the vinegar, open it up and remove the filling. Slice the marrow into good chunks and pack in jars. Then boil up the vinegar once more, this time with the sugar, and pour it hot over the pieces of marrow. Cover well and store in a cool dry place, preferably out of the light.

Marrow mangoes should be stored at least 3 months before opening. The interesting thing about the pickle is the variation in taste of different pieces. Some have an overpowering hot taste, while others are milder, with just a hint of onion flavour. But it's quite random, depending on the way the spices have been placed inside the marrow. Eat marrow mangoes either with cold meat or as a side dish with Indian food.

David Mabey

Pepper Relish

(Makes 2½ lb) (1.15 kg)

This is a recipe from a pickle feature published in *Woman* magazine. It is very quick to make and keeps well. Quite hot and spicy, it is excellent with cheese and cold meats.

6 medium red peppers
8 red or green chillies
1 lb tomatoes (450 g)
½ lb onions (225 g)
½ lb cooking apples (225 g)
1 level dessertspoon salt
¾ pint brown malt vinegar (425 ml)
½ lb granulated sugar (225 g)

Discard core and seeds from peppers and chillies. Cut peppers into quarters. Cover tomatoes with boiling water for 30 seconds. Drain and skin. Peel and quarter onions and apples.

Coarsely mince prepared ingredients. Put in a pan with the remaining ingredients. Bring to the boil and simmer until thick. Pot and cover.

Frances M. Waldett

Pumpkin and Tomato
Chutney
(Makes about 3½ lb) (1.5 kg)

It is not generally known that pumpkin can make an excellent chutney, rich and dark. The recipe below produces a mixture with a taste which is spicy but not too sharp; the pumpkin slices retain something of their shape, and shine translucently through the glass jars.

Greengrocers very often sell pumpkins by the piece. A whole one is of course cheaper, but remember that once it is cut it will not keep longer than about ten days.

a piece of pumpkin weighing about 2½ lb (gross weight) (1.15 kg)
1 lb ripe tomatoes (450 g)
½ lb onions (225 g)
2 oz sultanas (50 g)
¾ lb soft dark brown sugar (350 g)
¾ lb caster sugar (350 g)
2 tablespoons salt
2 scant teaspoons each of ground ginger, black peppercorns and
    allspice berries
2 cloves garlic
1¼ pints white, red or rosé wine vinegar or cider vinegar (720 ml)

Peel the pumpkin, discard seeds and cottony centre. Slice, then cut into pieces roughly 2 inches square (5 cm) and ½ inch thick (1 cm). Pour boiling water over the tomatoes, skin and slice them. Peel and slice the onions and the garlic.

Put all solid ingredients, including spices (crush the peppercorns and allspice berries in a mortar) and sugar, in your preserving pan. (For chutneys always use heavy aluminium, never untinned copper pans.) Add the vinegar. Bring gently to the boil and then cook steadily, but not at a gallop, until the mixture is jammy. Skim from time to time, and towards the end of the cooking, which will take altogether about 50 minutes, stir very frequently. Chutney can be a disastrous sticker if you don't give it your full attention during the final stages.

This is a long-keeping chutney but, like most chutneys, it is best if cooked to a moderate set only; in other words it should still be a little bit runny; if too solid it will quickly dry up.

Ladle into pots, which should be filled right to the brim. When cold cover with rounds of waxed paper, and then with Porosan skin or a double layer of thick greaseproof paper. Transparent covers which let in the light are not suitable for chutney.

The yield from these quantities will be approximately 3½ lb (1.5 kg); and although it may be a little more extravagant as regards fuel and materials, I find chutney cooked in small batches more satisfactory then when produced on a large scale.

It is worth noting that should it be more convenient, all ingredients for the chutney can be prepared, mixed with the sugar and vinegar, and left for several hours or overnight (but not longer than 12 hours) in a covered bowl before cooking.

Elizabeth David

Rhubarb Chutney (Makes about 6 lb) (2.7 kg)

One of the less usual chutney ingredients, but it makes a tasty mixture and is one way of using the enormous quantities of rhubarb that keep growing right through the summer. The large coarser stalks are perfect for this.

6 lb rhubarb (2.7 kg)
1 lb onions (450 g)
2 cloves garlic
2 tablespoons ground mixed spice
1 tablespoon salt
2 pints malt vinegar (1.15 litres)
2 lb preserving sugar (900 g)

225

Remove the roots and leaves from the rhubarb and wipe the stalks. Slice them and put them in a large pan. Skin and finely chop the onions and cloves of garlic and add them to the pan with the spice, salt and half of the vinegar. Bring to the boil, then reduce the heat and simmer the mixture until the rhubarb is very soft. Stir in the sugar and the remaining vinegar and when the sugar has completely dissolved, simmer the mixture until it is thick, stirring it frequently. Pour into hot clean jars, cover with Porosan skin or with pieces of linen, brushing the linen with melted candle wax to give an airtight seal. Label and store in a cool dark place.

Kathie Webber

Green Tomato Sour

This is in fact not sour at all, but very sweet and mellow.

6 lb small green tomatoes (2.7 kg)
2 lb onions (900 g)
3 green peppers
1½ lb brown sugar (700 g)
salt
3 tablespoons mustard seed
1 tablespoon or more coriander seed
2 tablespoons celery seed
2 pints vinegar, preferably spiced vinegar (1.15 litres)

Slice the tomatoes thinly and chop the onions. Put them in layers in a large earthenware bowl, sprinkling each layer with plenty of salt. Let them stand overnight, then drain off the liquid and put the tomatoes, onions, chopped green peppers, sugar, spices and vinegar in a preserving pan; the vinegar should barely cover the vegetables. Simmer for 2 hours, return the mixture to the bowl, allow to stand overnight, then simmer on until there is just enough liquid, which should be dark and thickish, to cover the vegetables when they are packed together.

Pour the chutney into clean hot jars, cover and keep three weeks at least before eating.

Caroline Conran.

Apple and Tomato Chutney

(Makes 4 lb) (1.8 kg)

Home grown tomatoes that are slow to ripen can be used for this recipe and the colour improved with two tablespoons of tomato purée.

2 lb apples (1 kg)
2 lb tomatoes (red) (1 kg)
2 lb onions (1 kg)
½ teaspoon salt
1 teaspoon black peppercorns, crushed
1 dessertspoon ground ginger
1½ pints white distilled vinegar (1 litre)
8 oz brown sugar (250 g)

Peel, core and slice the apples, tomatoes and onions. Put them in a bowl layered with the salt and spices and pour over the vinegar; cover and leave overnight.

Turn all together into a preserving pan, add the sugar, stir frequently and simmer until tender. Pour into hot jars and cover tightly when cold.

Rosemary Hume

227

About the Contributors

Alex Barker did the three year Home Economics Course at Isleworth Polytechnic and then joined the Home Economics and Recipe Development Department of Nestlé Foods. In 1972 she joined Buitoni Foods as their Home Economist and in 1973 joined *Woman's Own* as Assistant Cookery Editor and in 1975 took over as Cookery Editor. She thoroughly enjoys working for the magazine, creating new ideas, being involved with food photography and going out to visit readers—finding out what they would like to know and how to help them. She enjoys outdoor sport and has recently taken up hot air ballooning. She loves travelling and is involved with Task Force and Bacchus (Charity for Mentally Handicapped Children).

Mary Berry was born in Bath and studied cooking both there and in Paris. She now lives at Penn in Buckinghamshire with her husband and three young children and combines looking after her family with her cooking on Thames TV 'After Noon'. She is also Cooking Consultant to *Home and Freezer Digest Magazine*. She is the author of several books on cooking including *The All Colour Cook Book, Popular Freezer Cookery, Popular French Cookery* and *The Complete Book of Freezer Cooking*. Mary Berry has been Cookery Editor of various magazines including *Ideal Home* and *Housewife*. She made her first appearance on 'After Noon' in January 1973 and since then has presented many recipes on the programme.

Arabella Boxer was Food Correspondent for *Vogue* from 1966–8, and again from 1975 until now. She has written *First Slice Your Cookbook, A Second Slice, Arabella Boxer's Garden Cookbook* and *Christmas Food and Drink*; she has also edited *Seven Centuries of English Food* by Maxime McKendry. Winner of the 1975 Glenfiddich Award for Food Writer of the Year, she has also written for *The Sunday Times Magazine* and for *Nova*. A self-taught cook with no formal training, she is currently interested in primitive methods of cooking.

Robert Carrier is one of the world's most famous food writers. One time Food Editor of *The Sunday Times, Harper's Bazaar, Vogue* and *The Daily Telegraph Magazine*, he is now Food Editor of *Homes and Gardens*, and the author of *Great Dishes of the World, The Robert Carrier Cookbook, The Robert Carrier Cookery Course, Cooking for You* and more recently *Entertaining*. He seems purposely to have planned his life to enable him to explore the different cuisines of the world as thoroughly as possible. He was born in New York in 1923 and since then has travelled widely and studied French, Italian, German and Austrian cookery. He is now firmly settled in England where he has two famous restaurants, Carrier's in London and Hintlesham Hall in Suffolk. He is currently modernising an ancient Arab house in Marrakesh.

Caroline Conran was born in 1939. She went to Art School at Cambridge and her first jobs were as a waitress at Stockpot in London and doing room sets with and for Olive Sullivan. On to *Queen Magazine*, first as Drusilla Beyfus' assistant ('she being my mentor'), then as Home Editor. After her marriage to Terence Conran and the birth of her children she was a buyer for Habitat and then worked for Ernestine Carter on *The Sunday Times* ('very tough work'). She had three good years at *Nova*, working for four consecutive editors, and is still at *The Sunday Times*. She very much enjoyed writing *Poor Cook* and *Family Cook* with her friend Susan Campbell and is now writing for Marks and Spencer and translating a second book by Michel Guerard, following the success of her translation of *Cuisine Minceur*.

Margaret Coombes holds a wide interest in the culinary field through catering, demonstration and advertising and is the Good Housekeeping Institute's Director of Food and Cookery. Today, *The Good Housekeeping Cookery Book, Round the Year Menus, Home Freezer Cook Book* and *Home Baking* are just a few of the many bestselling titles to which she has contributed. Her creative expertise and flair for food photography are enjoyed by many thousands of enthusiastic *Good Housekeeping* magazine readers. Living in Surrey, Margaret runs her own home, devoting free time in a busy life to growing vegetables amongst the flowers. She strongly believes that fine food need not necessarily be expensive—selective buying, skilful preparation, an eye for simple presentation add up to good eating.

Magaret Costa was born in Rhodesia in 1917. She insisted on learning to cook and spent her first pocket money on a book called *Anyone Can Cook* and a tin of Royal Baking Powder. She won a scholarship to Lady Margaret Hall, Oxford, read Mediaeval French and ran the Ambassadors Theatre during the war. She joined *The Sunday Pictorial* (now *The Sunday Mirror*) and became Cookery Editor of *Everywoman, Modern Living* and *The Farmer and Stockbreeder,* then wine writer for *Housewife*. She succeeded Elizabeth David on *The Sunday Times* women's page and became first Food Editor, then Wine Editor, of *The Sunday Times Magazine*. She is now wine writer for *Woman's Journal* and has written for many other publications in Britain and America. She is married to Bill Lacy, formerly head chef at the Empress restaurant in Mayfair, and they started their own restaurant, Lacy's, in 1970. She has published *The Country Cook* and *The Four Seasons Cookery Book* and, in the US, *London at Table*.

Philippa Davenport used to be a Cookery Editor for IPC magazines and Marshall Cavendish, and the latter published her book *Good Cooking on a Budget*. She has been Cookery Correspondent for *The Financial Times* since 1973, and is Consultant Editor to Marshall Cavendish, for whom she recently created the partwork series *Good Cooking*. She feels that while most people are quite modest in their eating habits today, 'all too often there is a sharp division between the dishes we give our families and what we deem suitable to offer guests. This seems to me foolish and quite unnecessary; and I'm all for more frequent and more informal entertaining. The recipes I have chosen for this book aren't rock bottom cheap but neither are they extravagant. They are the sort of simple but good tasting foods that I like to relax over and share with family and friends'.

Elizabeth David became interested in good food and wine when living with a French family while she studied French history and literature at the Sorbonne in Paris. On her return to England she decided to teach herself to cook, in order to reproduce the delicious food she had learned to appreciate in France. Ever since then she has been a keen student of both the practical side and the literature of cookery, setting up her own kitchen in Italy, Greece, Egypt and India as well as France, learning the local dishes and reproducing them for herself. Her first book, *Mediterranean Food*, was published in 1950, and since then she has written and published *French Country Cooking, Italian Food* (which was a Book Society recommendation), *Summer Cooking, French Provincial Cooking* and *Spices, Salt and Aromatics in the English Kitchen*. Her latest book is *English Bread and Yeast Cookery*. In 1976 Mrs David was awarded the OBE and in 1977 was made Chevalier of the Ordre du Mérite Agricole.

Josceline Dimbleby was born in Oxford in 1943 and brought up abroad, mainly in the Middle East and South America, so that at an early age she learned to appreciate strong, unusual flavours and the use of herbs and spices in food. After school she trained as a singer, an occupation she tries to keep up as a complete contrast to cooking. Her instinct has always been to create her own dishes and she learned to cook through the trial and error of her own concoctions. She wrote *A Taste of Dreams* for friends who urged her to write down the dishes she made for them. This led to regular cookery pieces for *The Daily Mail* and a little book *Party Pieces* for the Victoria and Albert Museum's Silver Jubilee Exhibition. She is working on a new book, and lives in London with her husband David, and three lively, greedy young children whose appreciation of her food is a constant encouragement.

Muriel Downes is the Cordon Bleu Cookery School's co-principal with Rosemary Hume. Before the war she was a food specialist in Unilever's experimental kitchens. She joined the school when it re-opened in 1945 and with her great interest in French food, has travelled all over the world demonstrating the Cordon Bleu techniques and lecturing on the London school's cooking methods.

Gail Duff has been a cookery writer for four years, has published *Fresh All the Year* and *Gail Duff's Vegetarian Cookbook* and is working on a *Economy Cookbook*. She has contributed to *Homes and Gardens* and is Cookery Writer for *Vole*. She always uses fresh and natural ingredients and, although not a vegetarian would consider herself a 'food reformer'. She demonstrates all aspects of wholefood cookery for *Here's Health* magazine's 'Living Naturally' courses and to local societies. Her other main interests are the countryside, conservation and folk history and as she lives in Kent she has written on these subjects for *Kent Life* and BBC Radio Medway. She has just completed *The Country Wisdom Book*.

Rose Elliot was inspired to write her first cookery book, *Simply Delicious*, after helping out with the cookery at a vegetarian retreat centre. This led to further books, including *Not Just a Load of Old Lentils* and *The Oxfam Vegetable Cook Book*, and journalism. She lives in Hampshire with her husband and two daughters and combines cookery writing with looking after home and family. She specialises in vegetarian and wholefood cookery and is very interested in the health, nutritional and ecological aspects of cookery. Other interests include astrology (in which she is qualified as a consultant), psychology, theatre and amateur dramatics, classical music, dressmaking, sailing and painting.

Jane Grigson was born in 1928 and brought up in the north-east of England. She read English at Cambridge and then worked in art galleries, hoping to end up in the Victoria and Albert. When her fifth application was unsuccessful she turned to publishing and worked as assistant to the poet and critic Geoffrey Grigson, whom she later married, and then as a translator from French and Italian. She fell into cookery writing by accident, when a friend was unable to fulfil a contract for a book on charcuterie. She started writing for *The Observer Colour Magazine* in 1968, on Elizabeth David's recommendation. Her interests are English, French and Mediterranean cookery, with special reference to their history and the origins of foods and dishes generally.

Pamela Harlech was born and raised in New York City, has lived in England for fifteen years and is now married to the former British Ambassador to the United States. She has worked on *Vogue* magazines on both sides of the Atlantic as a

Feature Editor, as London Editor for American *Vogue* and Contributing Editor to British *Vogue* writing a recipe column, until 1975 when she began to write a news column on everything to do with food—from gadgets to ingredients. Author of *Feast Without Fuss*, Lady Harlech also writes freelance for *The Daily Mail*.

Rosemary Hume graduated from the Cordon Bleu in Paris and in the 1930s opened her own school called Au Petit Cordon Bleu in London. It was closed in World War II but re-opened in 1945 as the Cordon Bleu Cookery School. She was awarded the MBE in 1970 and presented with the André Simon award by her colleagues in the cooking profession in 1974.

Prue Leith, 38, divides her time between her School of Food and Wine in Notting Hill Gate, taking sixty students at a time; her City catering company which delivers board-room lunches and caters for weddings and banquets; and her rather grand restaurant in North Kensington. She is also Cookery Correspondent for *The Sunday Express*, has written numerous cook books, broadcasts frequently on radio and television, and has a farm in Oxfordshire producing fresh vegetables for her businesses. She also has a husband, author Rayne Kruger; two young children; two horses; two donkeys, and two goats.

Caroline Liddell is a qualified Home Economist with wide experience of professional cooking—from food photography to working in the cookery department of a magazine. She has worked closely with Robert Carrier (devising recipes in his test kitchen) and with Delia Smith. She has written two cookery books, the latest of which was *Ulcer Superdiet*.

Kenneth Lo was born in Foochow, China. Since he came to this country he has been a 'perpetual student' (six years at Cambridge and London Universities and five years previously at Peking), a 'professional eater' (over a decade with the *Egon Ronay Guide* and *Good Food Guide*, and now Chairman of the Chinese Gourmet Club) in addition to having been a diplomat, welfare and industrial relations officer with the Chinese seamen in Liverpool, fine-art publisher, lecturer, broadcaster and professional tennis player. He has written more books on Chinese food and cooking than anybody in the world, several of them bestsellers. Best known are *Chinese Food, Quick and Easy Chinese Cooking, Cheap Chow, Encyclopedia of Chinese Cookery, Peking Cooking, Chinese Vegetarian Cooking* and *Love of Chinese Cooking.*

David Mabey was born in Hertfordshire in 1947. He studied pharmacy at university, moved to East Anglia in 1970 and worked at many trades including gardener and hotel cook before embarking on writing full time. His books include *Breadlines, The Penguin Book of Jams, Pickles and Chutneys* and *The Vegetable Grower's Calendar.* He has just completed a book on preserving meat and fish and is currently working on a project dealing with regional food. He also contributes regularly to *Vole,* and does occasional lecturing and broadcasting.

Anna MacMiadhachain was born in Hampstead, went to school in Watford and later to the Art College. She worked then for the British Baking Industries at their research station at Chorley-wood. She married the painter Padraig MacMiadhachain in 1960 and shares the MacIntyre Saul Studio with him in Swanage, where they both exhibit their work. She has written *Spanish Regional Cookery,* also the Iberian section for Mitchell Beazley's *World Atlas of Food,* and a section of Spanish and Portuguese food for a new book to be published this year. Her interests are painting, travel, food and horses. She has two daughters.

Mary Meredith has been Cookery Editor of *Woman and Home* for 29 years. For 21 of those years she was Cookery Editor of *Woman's Weekly* too. Mary also directs the *Woman and Home* Cook Schools in London and Edinburgh. Although Mary was born and brought up in Broughty Ferry near Dundee she now lives in a small village in Surrey where she indulges in her hobbies of gardening and beekeeping. A family cottage in the Dordogne, means that Mary enjoys holidays in France where she also pursues her interest in French food. Mary Meredith has two cookery books to her credit and has worked on both radio and TV.

Frances Naldrett gained practical cookery experience the hard way—cooking for a hundred and fifty hungry boys in a school. She then went to Canada where she was Assistant to the Food Editor of the *Toronto Globe and Mail*. This gave her a special interest in American food and also the food of the immigrant population. On returning to England she was Home Economist in an advertising agency before going to *Family Circle* as Deputy Cookery Editor. Six years later she joined *Woman* magazine as Cookery Editor. She says: We try to make the cookery pages of *Woman* entertaining and informative as well as helpful to readers struggling to give their families nutritious and interesting meals in these days of rising prices'.

Marguerite Patten has the reputation of being 'Britain's best-selling cookery writer', for she has written over a hundred cookery books which sell in many countries. She is well-known for her cookery demonstrations all over Britain and her radio talks and television demonstrations. For many years she was responsible for the cookery demonstrations on BBC television afternoon programmes and had the rather grand title of President of the BBC Cookery Club. She has travelled round the world to learn about the foods and recipes of other countries. A little publicised aspect of her work is her lectures in training colleges, so she is kept very busy writing and talking about food.

Helena Radecka was born in Warsaw in 1939 and grew up with two different culinary traditions, those of her father's native Poland and Istanbul, where her mother was born. Her family came to Scotland after the war and she took an MA degree in English at the University of Edinburgh in 1960. She went into publishing and as the only female editor in the firm she was landed with its cookery list and went on to edit many bestselling cookery books. She also ran Robert Carrier's test kitchen for a while, researching and writing up recipes. She is now a consultant cookery editor, has written the cookery section of *Your Kitchen Garden* and is working on another book.

Evelyn Rose is a well-known writer, broadcaster and consultant in home economics and an authority on Jewish food and food customs. As Cookery Editor of the *Jewish Chronicle*—where she has a weekly recipe column—she demonstrates and lectures widely on the subject of Jewish food. She has contributed to many national newspapers and magazines and has had several television series. She is a consultant to several National Food Boards and major food firms. She is a past National Chairman of the Association of Home Economists, a member of the Consumers' Committee of the Meat and Livestock Commission, and sole consumer member of the Meat Promotion Committee. Evelyn Rose is married, with three children.

Delia Smith has become known to a wide and appreciative audience through her *Evening Standard* cookery column and her television series 'Family Fare' and 'Look East'. She is starting a major new BBC series this autumn. Her writing is distinguished by her practical approach to the problems of producing good food, and her book *Frugal Food* shows how the soaring cost of food and the dwindling resources of the planet provide the motivating force for a new and positive approach to cookery, a concern which is followed up with her special interest in *Food For Our Times*. Other publications include *How to Cheat at Cooking* and the recently successful *Delia Smith's Book of Cakes*.

Michael Smith trained at the International Hotel Schools in Lausanne and Paris. He writes for many publications in Britain and America, including *The New York Times*, *The Sunday Times*, *The Yorkshire Post*, *The Glasgow Herald* and *House and Garden*. He is a regular contributor to national radio stations, appears weekly on BBC television in his cookery spot 'Grace and Flavour' from Pebble Mill and was cookery advisor on the 'Upstairs, Downstairs' series and 'The Duchess of Duke Street'. He travels a great deal both here and abroad lecturing and giving classes and he also designs interiors for town and country houses and restaurants. Publications include *Fine English Cookery*, *The Best of British Cookware* and *The Duchess of Duke Street Entertains*.

Katie Stewart started work as a food journalist over fifteen years ago on returning from a stay in America. Her interest in food had taken her out to White Plains, New York a year or so earlier where she worked as a Home Economist in the test kitchens of a major American food company. Once home again, she had intended to continue her career in industry but the chance of journalism seemed too good an opportunity to miss. She started work on the now defunct *Woman's Mirror* in 1959 and eight years later graduated to *The Times* newspaper and *Woman's Journal* magazine.

Marika Hanbury Tenison (who is married to the explorer, Robin Hanbury Tenison) became interested in cooking at the age of eleven. She became the Cookery Editor of *The Sunday Telegraph* in 1967 and has produced numerous cookery books including *Soups and Hors d'Oeuvres, Eat Well and be Slim, Deep Freeze Cookery, Deep Freeze Sense, Left Over for Tomorrow, The Best of British Cooking* and *The Magimix Food Processor Cookery Book.* In 1977 she became expert in producing good food from the minimum of resources when she took on the role of cook to the Royal Geographical Society's Mulu Expedition to Sarawak in Borneo. She also writes as a freelance on cookery and travel, is Cookery Editor of *The Spectator* and does a certain amount of television and radio work.

Janet Warren originally trained as a Home Economist and then completed a course at the Cordon Bleu. She worked within the cookery department of two major woman's magazines, eventually taking responsibility for the cookery pages of *Woman's Weekly* and becoming at that time the youngest Cookery Editor in Fleet Street. She broadcasts often on radio and television and has written several cookery books, the most recent on *Pressure Cooking.* Her interests include gardening and sailing but she enjoys nothing better than going out to dinner. Recently, though, so she can spend more time at home with her baby son Simon, she has relinquished her position at *Woman's Weekly* to take over the Cookery Editorship of *Good Life, Woman's Weekly's* new monthly magazine.

Kathie Webber was born in Yorkshire, and growing up in a household where good plain fare was the norm, she started cooking as soon as she could reach the kitchen table. Cookery became a hobby and the hobby included training and subsequently adding various examination results (first class) to

238

her love of the subject. When the time came to mix cookery with journalism, the background to both subjects was well etched in. Currently, Kathie Webber is Cookery Editor for *TVTimes*, and having written a series of four books and completed a cookery card project this year, she's sitting at her typewriter with a blank piece of paper in front of her, trying to start her tenth cookery book.

Harold Wilshaw has at various times and for varying periods been chef, hotelier, restaurateur, lecturer, demonstrator and cookery journalist. He has written three books and contributed to as many more. He has a love-hate relationship with a typewriter, which is wearing thin, but 'needs must go on'.

Acknowledgments

Carrier, Robert. Caviar d'Aubergines, Creamed Finnan Haddie, Lamb Hash Parmentier, Oriental Rice Salad, Chocolate Beer Cake from ENTERTAINING (Sidgwick and Jackson, 1977).

Coombes, Margaret. Cheese Baked Eggs from GOOD HOUSE-KEEPING COOKING WITH HERBS AND SPICES (National Magazine Co. Ltd., 1975); Pasta in Soured Cream Sauce, Coconut Wafers from GOOD HOUSEKEEPING ROUND THE YEAR MENUS (National Magazine Co. Ltd., 1975); Kentish Chicken Pudding, Nut and Cream Cheese Bake, Spiced Cauliflower with Rice, Pear Caramel Roll from *Good Housekeeping Magazine*; Nig Nogs from GOOD HOUSEKEEPING COOKERY BOOK (National Magazine Co. Ltd., 1948, completely revised 1976).

Costa, Margaret. Goulash Soup, Smoked Haddock Soufflé, Bacon and Corned Beef Loaf, Paprika Potatoes, Rhubarb Charlotte from THE COUNTRY COOK (Farmer and Stockbreeder Publications Ltd., 1960).

Davenport, Philippa. Very Fishy Stew, Nutty Cabbage from GOOD COOKING ON A BUDGET (Marshall Cavendish, 1976); Beignets de Cervelle from *The Financial Times*.

David, Elizabeth. Potato Sausages from FRENCH PROVINCIAL COOKING (Michael Joseph, 1960, re-issued 1977; Penguin 1964); Pigeons Stewed with Lettuces, Pickled Plums from SUMMER COOKING (Museum Press, 1955; Penguin, 1965); Sour-Sweet Cabbage from ITALIAN FOOD (Macdonald, 1954; re-issued Allen Lane, 1977; Penguin, 1963); Pumpkin and Tomato Chutney from SPICES, SALT AND AROMATICS IN THE ENGLISH KITCHEN (Penguin, 1970).

Duff, Gail. Spinach and Curd Cheese Topping for Pasta, Barbecued Soya Beans from GAIL DUFF'S VEGETARIAN COOKBOOK (Macmillan London Ltd., 1978); Rabbit and

241

Celery in Cider from FRESH ALL THE YEAR (Pan Books, 1976).

Grigson, Jane. Curried Parsnip Soup from GOOD THINGS (Michael Joseph, 1971, Penguin, 1973).

Harlech, Pamela. Chicken Liver and Caper Pâté, My Mother's Chocolate Cake from FEAT WITHOUT FUSS (Cape, 1976).

Leith, Prudence. Beer Bread from Leith's School of Food and Wine's Beginners' Course.

Mabey, David. Marrow Mangoes from JAMS, PICKLES AND CHUTNEYS by David and Rose Mabey (Macmillan, 1975, Penguin, 1976).

Meredith, Mary. Cauliflower and Bacon Flan, Fish Slice, Fore-hock of Bacon, Lapin Provençal from *Woman and Home* Cook Schools.

Naldrett, Frances. Pepper Relish from *Woman*.

Patten, Marguerite. Sillsalat from CLASSIC DISHES MADE SIMPLE (Hamlyn, 1969).

Radecka, Helena. Runner Beans à la Grecque, Spinach Cutlets, Mustard Glazed Turnips, Haricot Beans from YOUR KITCHEN GARDEN (Mitchell Beazley Publishers Ltd., 1975).

Rose, Evelyn. Chicken and Tomato Soup from MORE RECIPES FROM LOOK NORTH (BBC Publications, 1977); Plum Kuchen, Spiced Cherry Jam from THE COMPLETE INTER-NATIONAL JEWISH COOKBOOK (Robson Books, 1976). 1976).

Smith, Delia. Kippery Kedgeree, Meatballs with Peppers and Tomatoes, Barbecued Pork Slices, Turkish Stuffed Peppers, Pears in Cider from RECIPES FROM LOOK EAST 3 (BBC Publications, 1977).

Smith, Michael. Turnep Soup from FINE ENGLISH COOKERY (Faber, 1973); Melon and Cassia Bud Salad, Chocolate Soufflé from MORE GRACE AND FLAVOUR (BBC Publications, 1977); Creamed Kidneys with Ginger from THE DUCHESS OF DUKE STREET ENTERTAINS, (W. H. Allen, 1977); Solomongundi from GRACE AND FLAVOUR (BBC Publications, 1977).

Tenison, Marika Hanbury. Avocado and Cucumber Soup from EAT WELL AND BE SLIM (Pan Books, 1974); West Coast Fish Stew, Tickler's Pie from THE BEST OF BRITISH COOKING (Hart-Davis, MacGibbon, 1976).

A Note from Oxfam

Buying this book is one way of helping Oxfam's work overseas. There are other ways, however, in which you may consider helping – such as buying handicrafts and gifts from Oxfam shops or donating items, sending Oxfam christmas cards, knitting blanket squares or by making regular donations. This can be done by filling in and cutting out, or copying, the banker's order or covenant form below. Please return to Oxfam, 274 Banbury Road, Oxford.

Banker's order   AP.1

To the Manager .... (Name of bank)

at .... (Address of bank)

....

Please pay Oxfam £   every month/year

starting on .... *(date) until further notice*

Name ....

Address ....

....

....

Signed ....

To Barclays Bank, High Street, Oxford (20 65 31) Account 60646792/60646784
quoting our reference

My covenant to Oxfam   AP.1

I .... Mr/Mrs/Miss
                   FULL NAME IN BLOCK CAPITALS PLEASE

of .... (address)

....

undertake to pay Oxfam each year for seven years (or during my lifetime if shorter) from today, the sum that will, after the deduction of income tax at the basic rate be £

date .... Signed and sealed...................................

To complete this covenant your signature requires a witness.

Witnesses signature ....

Witnesses address

*Just put here the amount you wish to pay annually and we do the rest

245

Send for Oxfam's mail order catalogue of handicrafts and gifts from Third World producers from Bridge, 274 Banbury Road, Oxford.

Please write to your Oxfam Regional Office for any further information about Oxfam's work and how you can help (address in your local telephone directory), or write to the Information Department at the Oxford address printed above.

Index